THE FUTURE OF SOUTH AFRICA

THE FUTURE
OF SOUTH AFRICA

A Study by British Christians

Published for the
British Council of Churches by
SCM PRESS LTD
BLOOMSBURY STREET LONDON

FIRST PUBLISHED 1965
© BRITISH COUNCIL OF CHURCHES 1965
PRINTED IN GREAT BRITAIN BY
BILLING AND SONS LTD
GUILDFORD AND LONDON

CONTENTS

I

PREFACE BY THE EDITORS

(December 1964)

This Report is published at the beginning of a year during which Britain will take fundamental decisions concerning her policy towards South Africa. The occasions will be, first the presentation to the Security Council of the Report being prepared on the feasibility of sanctions, and second, the judgment of the International Court of Justice concerning South-West Africa. Within the Security Council, Britain will be at the focal point of decision.

Christians will rightly expect the Government to take full account of the deep moral issues involved. Equally, Christians have a duty to study the facts if their concern for those moral issues is to be given weight. It was for this reason that the British Council of Churches instructed its International Department to make a special study of the two issues of sanctions and South-West Africa, as part of a larger study of the problems connected with South Africa and the future of all her people. Accordingly, a special Working Party prepared the present Report, between November, 1963 and September, 1964. It is now made available for study within the Churches.

Since its presentation to the Council in October there have been two developments of which note must be taken in reading the Report. The first was the decision of the new Government to place an embargo on new contracts for the supply of arms to South Africa, but to permit the sale of the Buccaneer aircraft already ordered. The second was the decision of the South African Government to suspend the '90-day' detention clause as from January, 1965.

From the nature of its commissioning the Report was written for Christians in Britain. The members of the Working Party sought within the severe limits of communication between the races in South Africa constantly to correct their initial viewpoints. The Report seeks to reflect the position they reached. It is our hope that Christians of all races in South Africa will comment on the points at which both the descriptive sections and the conclusions may fail to do justice to the situation they experience.

The Working Party was a group of Christians making an attempt to grapple honestly with the political, legal and economic intricacies involved. The result is offered as a contribution to the study of a complex and intractable problem, the solution of which will directly affect future peace in Southern Africa and the future of the Church throughout the Continent.

T. A. Beetham, *Chairman of the Working Party*
Noël Salter, *Secretary of the Working Party*

2

Resolution adopted by the British Council of Churches on 20th October 1964

The Council resolved in the following terms:

1. The Council receives the report on 'The Future of South Africa', expresses its gratitude to the members of the working party which prepared it, commends it to the member Churches, and hopes that it may be made available to the public by publication in printed form;

2. The Council, while not regarding economic sanctions at this stage as likely to lead to a satisfactory solution of the South African problem, requests Her Majesty's Government as a matter of urgency to consider what measures are required to ensure that Britain and her citizens no longer act in such a way as to encourage *apartheid*;

3. The Council resolves that an early opportunity be sought to lay before the Foreign Secretary the report on 'The Future of South Africa' and the resolutions of the Council arising therefrom, and to discuss with him British policy towards South Africa;[1]

4. The Council instructs the International Department to keep under review the matters dealt with in the working party's enquiry, and to report further to the Council following the report of the United Nations' Committee set up by the Security Council to consider 'the feasibility, effectiveness and implications of measures which could, as appropriate, be taken by the Security Council under the United Nations' Charter', and following the judgment of the International Court of Justice concerning South-West Africa.

[1] The Foreign Secretary received a delegation led by the Bishop of Chichester on 3rd December 1964.

3

INTRODUCTION

1. We were asked by the British Council of Churches to study the problems connected with the future of South Africa, in particular the issues of sanctions and South-West Africa. This led the Working Party not only to consider the moral issues involved, but also the relevant economic, legal and military considerations. Nor could the study be made without taking account of the position of the High Commission Territories. The whole was preceded by an analysis of many aspects of *apartheid* legislation as it at present affects the lives of men and women in South Africa. The result was necessarily a lengthy study.

2. This introduction briefly describes the tenor of our thinking and our concluding judgments. Such a summary, however, inevitably omits many elements essential to a fair appraisal of a complex situation, and we would not wish this introduction to be considered separately from the Report itself.

3. Our study affirms that the personal indignities, the educational and economic restrictions and the almost total lack of civic and political rights as citizens of the Republic suffered by the non-whites of South Africa call for redress. We recognize that we who are white do not appreciate readily the effect of affronts to the individual because of the colour of his skin; we therefore commend the words of Dr Luther King in Appendix III of the Report. Everything in the lives of non-whites in South Africa, the separated areas in which they live, the type of education available to their children, the total lack of participation in the government of their country, spells for thirteen and a half million of the seventeen million inhabitants of the Republic a second-class status. That in such circumstances many carry a cheerful face and no hard bitterness of heart must not be taken as indicating that they are content for things to remain as they are.

> Because my mouth is wide with laughter and my throat is deep with song,
> You do not think I suffer after I have held my pain so long.

4. To see the situation thus through the eyes of the African majority of their land is something which as yet only a tiny minority of white

South Africans are willing to do. Yet as it is the three million white people who hold the political, economic and social power, it is upon them that immediate responsibility in South Africa rests. It is their thought and action which it is most necessary to influence at this juncture; yet they are critical of any outside attempts to assess the problems they face.

5. This is the dilemma facing the universal Church. African Christians in South Africa look to the world-wide Church, as to the Church in their country, for action and not only words; fundamentally, Christians believe in mutual discussion, not forceful pressure; yet even an attempt to assess the restrictions under which non-whites live, let alone any suggestion for improving their position, is regarded by the majority of white Christians in South Africa as so unjustified an attitude as to render impossible that reaching out in fellowship as we should wish.

6. That Christians in Britain should believe that white Christians in South Africa are failing in obedience to Jesus Christ is to them a surprise. They compare our empty churches with their full ones; they refer to declining moral standards in Britain, are shocked at the holiday hooliganism of our 'mods' and 'rockers'. We may consider such arguments to be irrelevant: it is still needful to take this attitude among white South Africans into account, if they are to begin to listen to what we may have to say.

7. Our answer to the question, 'Why pay special attention to South Africa, when human rights are violated in many parts of the world?' is given in Section II of the Report. An essential point is our special involvement in the present situation in South Africa. We believe it could lead to a world conflict in which the people of this country would be directly involved.

8. At a deeper level, we must recognize that we ourselves are directly bound up in the sinfulness of the present racial situation in South Africa. What is done there presents in an exacerbated form the same kind of failures as we show within our own society; moreover, the relation of races to each other is now a basic problem facing all humanity.

9. This sense of common involvement, of sinfulness shared, that if 'one part suffer, all suffer' is true of British Christians to a special degree. The role played by Britain, and people of British stock, in the making of South Africa, not least in the building up of the Christian Church, is unique. English is still the mother tongue of nearly half the white population of the country. The United Kingdom is far and away her major trading partner.

10. Yet for all this, it is not we in Britain who today have to bear the cross of reconciliation. The outcome of the deepening crisis in South Africa will be decisive for all her citizens: for most of us in Britain it will be limited to vicarious experience.

11. In paragraph 3, we showed our starting point to be the situation of the oppressed races in all its hopelessness. Into the depth of this none but an African can fully enter. We hope the sober portrayal of facts and statistics in Section V of the Report will stimulate and not lull the effort of imagination and sympathy which it is our duty to make.

12. Nevertheless, if any policy is to lead to reconciliation, it must enter into the sense of doom, the deep anxiety and insecurity haunting many realistic white South Africans who, humanly speaking, can see no future for their children. The attitude of the South African white is characterized, not primarily by hate, but by fear. It is not physical fear in the first case, but fear of being 'ploughed under and submerged'. When we consider that the proportion of non-white to white persons in South Africa is forty times greater than in the U.S.A., it is justice to recognize that separate development is the kind of defence mechanism which would probably be tried by most groups believing themselves to be faced with the possibility of being swamped by overwhelming numbers of another group.

13. We have therefore to eschew any spirit of self-righteousness, while speaking the truth as we see it, in humility. There is need for compassion for the fate of *all* races. There is also need for realism. The situation is stark; in the view of some, it has almost reached the point of no return. Hence, it is prudent to prepare for radical action.

I. THE FACTS

14. Section V of the Report attempts to analyse the way in which *apartheid*, or separate development, is being worked out today. In doing so it describes the intensity of Afrikaner nationalism which inspired the long struggle of a settler group to become a nation, and which today carries most white South African opinion with it in insisting on racial segregation. The Section concludes (para. 51)—though it does not state the time-scale for the consequence—

> The total effect is one of inexorable compression creating conditions for a general explosion.

15. The historical steps by which this position was reached may be delineated, but this does not remove the fact that in the world of 1964 no human group in Africa or elsewhere will passively accept a future according to a pattern that has been prescribed by others.

16. The reality of *apartheid* is not of Africans living in homelands where they enjoy an increasing measure of independence and self-realization within a traditional tribal pattern, but a voteless urban proletariat, which constantly increases in numbers as economic suction draws them from the reserves. The figures published by the South African Government in January of this year show that between 1951

Facts - Reality of apartheid

Economic boom would colapse with out African Labour.

and 1960 the African urban population actually increased by more than one million, or over 40 per cent. As a result, today 60 per cent of all Africans live in the white areas.

17. Thus the dilemma of the white South African is that of unacceptable alternatives. The whole structure of his society depends on the economic integration of Africans. Yet its corollary: political and social integration, he will not accept.

18. In practice, therefore, 'separate development' means that the minority of Africans are separated in the Bantustans, while the majority, who live in the 87 per cent of the country which constitutes the 'white' areas, are segregated and discriminated against daily. *With regard to the central issue of African labour and residence in the urban areas, the Bantustan policy is the pursuit of the irrelevant.*

19. Meanwhile urban Africans suffer outrages to their personal and family life which are added to each year by fresh legislation. How real these are may be seen from Pastor Mvusi's moving address to the Christian Council of South Africa in May.[1] These oppressive measures are necessary corollaries of separate development. The South African Government is as aware of the figures given in paragraph 16 as it is of the fact that industry—and the current economic boom—would collapse without African labour. It therefore seeks to square the circle by:

(a) Limiting the total number of Africans in the urban areas by 'influx control';

(b) Reducing those who do live in the townships to the status of mobile labour digits, whom it is sought to shunt back to the reserves peridocially to prevent them establishing any acquired rights of family or residence;

(c) Corralling off this labour force in townships which may provide superior standards of accommodation, but an essential function of which is to make easier the group control of the inmates.

It is difficult for any white man to enter into the total effect on the personal lives of Africans of the mass of laws by which these ends are sought.

20. It is therefore misleading simply to characterize the pattern in South Africa as that of a white entrepreneurial element and an evolving black sub-citizenry, who are discriminated against in ownership of property, entry into jobs, wage scales and education. Prohibited by law from organizing unions, bargaining collectively, striking or moving freely, the African is obliged to sell his labour at an unjust price. The true ethos of the system is that of three million whites whose standard of living depends on seven million economic helots. As in Sparta 2,500

[1] See Appendix VIII of the Report. Cf. also 'Residence Permits in Towns' (Appendix VII), p. 113.

years ago, the latter have no political rights, but are kept subservient by habit, hunger, resignation or the threat of force.

21. One further comment can be made: once secondary education was given to the Africans—totally inadequate though this still is[1]—the possibility of maintaining such a system in the long run was destroyed.

22. It is not surprising that this situation, and the unrest and sabotage to which it gives rise, is not hermetically sealed within South Africa. If there is one thing for which in the long run the rest of Africa may unite its efforts, it is a crusade to liberate their oppressed brethren in the southern tip of the continent. As the new African states enter their era of independence, to many *apartheid* is, in the words of the Secretary-General of the Organization of African Unity,

> the most abominable symbol of the worst humiliations that the centuries have imposed upon Africa.

It is true that the military logistics of the present situation[2] make it unrealistic to envisage the Addis Ababa powers pitting their small and unco-ordinated armed forces, over great distances through difficult terrain without adequate lines of communication, against the modern air and land forces of South Africa. But the crusade now being prepared will not be held back by material odds. Once the protective ring of buffer states has been breached, subversive elements (whose training has already begun) will increasingly be passed across the frontier, and there are likely to be frontier incidents and raids. There will be a risk of increasing para-military involvement of the Eastern and Western blocs, with the real possibility of world conflict to which a magnified Congo-type situation could lead. Action by the United Nations is called for, not least because a race war, once started, could scarcely be confined to the African continent. This bell could toll for us all.

23. *Apartheid* is a grievous hindrance to the Gospel in Africa. There will be little hope of winning the post-independence generation of young Africans for Jesus Christ if the white Churches, within and without South Africa, are more loyal to their whiteness than to the Cross. Muslim missionaries are able to claim that it is Islam and not Christianity which offers brotherhood to Africans. Whether Christianity or Islam wins the heart of Africa (and one in three people in Africa is today a Muslim) could depend on the Christian witness—and suffering with the oppressed—in South Africa.

24. It is not possible to evade or blur the issue. What Africans claim in South Africa is in large measure the result of what they have learned of the Christian view of man and society. Southern Africa's contemporary African leaders were nearly all educated in Christian schools.

[1] See Appendix VI of the Report, p. 105.
[2] See paras. 75–78 and Appendix XII of the Report, p. 127.

25. There is a disquieting element of truth in the view that separate development in South Africa began within the Church, and spread from thence into the body politic. If today the ordinary white members of all the Churches joined their leaders in practical and courageous witness to the truth that God made all men of one blood, the results would be incalculable. In South Africa there are more than seven million Christians, of whom four and a half million are Africans and two and a half million are whites. Who can say this constitutes no ground for hope?

II. THE ALTERNATIVES BEFORE SOUTH AFRICA

26. The world needs Africa: Africa needs South Africa: South Africa needs a settlement that will not be a source of permanent resentment, 'accepted' by one side only as a stepping-stone to more later on. No alternative proposed to 'separate development' as at present practised can be given Christian support, unless it has taken into account the fears and hopes of all ethnic groups and has a substantial basis of support within each. They have not merely to live within it and make it function, but to find opportunity within it for using the talents which God has given them. This does not exclude an evolutionary element being built into such a settlement.

27. The point of departure must be the facts as they are. As shown in Section V of the Report, there is a single economic society. In five main employment divisions—mining, manufacturing, construction, railways and post office—nearly three times as many non-whites as whites are employed. To envisage splitting this single economic unit is to envisage the economic non-sense of splitting the factors of production: management and capital, labour and raw materials. Of these, neither raw materials, nor most of the existing capital plant, buildings, etc., are mobile. Those accustomed to thinking in political rather than in economic categories do not always sufficiently appreciate the control over all our lives exercised by the conditions of production. To destroy these conditions would mean destroying the present structure of South Africa. It is therefore unthinkable in terms of consent, though a solution may involve far-reaching modifications.

28. The basic consent problem may be formulated thus:

> *How do you establish justice for the non-white majority of the people while at the same time ensuring security for the white minority?*

29. It follows from paras. 17 and 27 above that the only way forward is to accept that economic integration cannot be indefinitely divorced from political and social integration. At this point we meet the historical situation in South Africa, where such integration means transforming a dominant minority within a larger whole into a minority whose position depends, not on legal discrimination, but on its own competitive abili-

ties, which are a function of higher education and greater technological experience. For this to be based on consent, there can be no question of subjection of any one ethnic group to another, but a common contribution to a South Africa which has a unique contribution to make as the industrial leader of Africa as a whole.

30. Given that a settlement could subsequently be changed by parliament; given the principle of one man one vote; given the ratio of four Africans to one white, it is understandable that a white South African writer has asked:

> Where on earth will you find a racial or other group of three million highly educated and developed people who, having for three centuries ruled the country and built up a great material civilization, will voluntarily vote themselves into another group, or just hand over under conditions such as prevail in South Africa today? No policy which does not *guarantee* or seem permanently to guarantee the security of the white group will be acceptable to them as a group.[1]

31. Such is the background against which the Working Party examined the three other possible patterns to the present—Christianly unacceptable—pattern of white domination described in the Report. What follows is a brief comment, as indicated in the second paragraph of this Introduction.

Partition

32. The Working Party cannot commend outright partition as a solution, because it seems impossible to establish except by force and bloodshed, and would contain within it the dragon's teeth of later strife. By outright partition is meant complete separation of white from black, leaving, for instance, a white rump state in the Western Cape.

33. Such a denial of the facts of history and economic life is rejected by both Africans and whites in South Africa alike, because both believe—correctly—that the land is theirs. For without either, it would not be the South Africa of today, which man has wrested from nature during three centuries in which the toil and blood of all races have been poured out together.

34. On this subject, an expert committee of the United Nations reported in April 1964:[2]

> No line of partition could be established by agreement, and an imposed partition would create a long frontier of continuing conflict. Nor could partition be politically or economically viable, for there is

[1] Prof. Ben Marais, *The Two Faces of Africa*, Shuter and Shooter, Pietermaritzburg, 1964, p. 62.
[2] Para. 26. See Appendix II, para. 2 (2), p. 99.

no substantial area of South Africa in which there is a majority of whites, and the economy of South Africa, both in industry and agriculture, is entirely dependent on non-white labour. Partition would not solve, but would intensify and aggravate, racial conflict.

A Non-racial State

35. While a non-racial state is the most desirable ultimate solution, the Working Party is fully conscious of the impossibility of this being established immediately in South Africa with the consent of the white minority.

36. Elements which would have to be taken into account in any move towards a non-racial unitary state include the following:

(1) Africans must feel that any solution is one they have shared in making, not one 'dished out to them by the whites'. Much of the present resentment derives from the sense of being treated as children. To them a hundred Baragwanath hospitals can be no substitute for participation in democratic decision-making.

(2) In spite of the claim of the politically conscious African leaders for 'one man one vote today *not* tomorrow', an evolutionary element might be acceptable to many Africans—*provided* that the time-scale were clearly defined and the initial step sufficiently decisive. In the end, not only the political but the total human approach of the white group to the other groups will be decisive.

(3) The present fear-ridden South African situation excludes a self-contained solution. Any solution by consent always requires faith in each other's motives and intentions, since all written documents can be evaded or abrogated. The only possibility is to find external points of anchorage. In the present total African situation, an element in the security of South African minority ethnic groups can only come from outside Africa. This means convincing the whites of the preparedness of the Americans and the British to intervene jointly, not only now but in the future, in order to uphold any agreed settlement. The form such a guarantee might take—no doubt through the United Nations, and relating to a Bill of Rights—is less important than the principle of guarantee. If enough confidence could be generated for such a guarantee to be both credible and acceptable to white and black in South Africa, the *casus foederis* would probably never arise.

A Federal Solution?

37. Faced with the difficulty of integration by consent, and the unacceptability of partition by force, many have envisaged some form of more limited association, which would preserve the essentials of a single

B

economic unit, yet allow for some regional differentiation of racial groups.

38. By an appropriate drawing of boundaries, most of the states which composed a federal or confederal system would comprise a large majority of one racial group, while some, in particular the highly industrialized Rand, would be designated 'non-racial'. The main characteristics of the majority of any state would thus be able to find expression within its internal government, educational system and pattern of social development. Human and ethnic rights would be guaranteed in the federal constitution, and minority fears could be further assuaged through a system of weighted representation in the federal parliament.

39. The important thing about any system that stands between a unitary state and two states (partition) is that it should correspond to the degree of will to be united, though not unitary. This in turn will reflect the appreciation by the ethnic groups concerned of their mutual interest, and the in-built historical conditioning of the existing situation. It could well be that the application of the federal principle to the racial situation in South Africa has within it the germ of an equitable and viable solution. (See the Report: paras. 65–9 and Appendix XIV.)

A South African Solution

40. While it is true that it would be irresponsible to criticize the policy of separate development without suggesting any alternative, only those who will have to live under the alternative system can decide its form. The voice of those who may be called upon to guarantee any solution can decide only the terms of that guarantee. A solution by consent supposes a conference of the leaders of their choice of all sections of the people of South Africa. This a South African government must call. The present South African Government will not do so until it has been brought to the point of recognizing that an alternative to *apartheid* must be found. To this end Christians in Britain should bend their efforts within both state and Church.

III. ACTION BY THE BRITISH GOVERNMENT

41. At this time a policy of immediate United Nations sanctions is being advocated as an alternative to the policy being followed by the British Government. *The Working Party believes neither of these to be the right course in present circumstances.*

A. *Policy of Connivance at* Apartheid

42. The present[1] policy of the British Government is to combine verbal denunciation of *apartheid* at the United Nations with practical encouragement of it, by maintaining normal trading relations with South

[1] Written before the General Election: see note on page 28.

Africa and supplying arms which could be used against United Nations units (including their British contingent) if U.N. action were decided upon. Recent exchanges in the House of Commons concerning arms to South Africa have obscured the fact that there is more difference of tone than of substance between the two main parties. The Government have already limited the export of arms; if they are returned to power in October, after the Buccaneer contract has been completed, it is to be hoped that they will refuse to grant any new contracts.[1] Thus the major difference compared with a Labour government is that the latter are committed to cancelling the important Buccaneer contract. What this whole domestic debate has obscured is that in conventional arms South Africa has already become largely self-supporting.[2] When it comes to any form of coercion of South Africa by economic sanctions, both Conservative and Labour leadership are hostile to them.

43. Thus the two main British political parties may both be considered guilty of affording indirect encouragement to *apartheid*, in so far as they are both opposed to sanctions, yet have no alternative to suggest. There is conclusive evidence how important to South Africa this encouragement is. It enables her to snap her fingers at the United Nations, and enjoy an economic boom because her key trading partners continue to take her goods. In this, of course, Britain is not alone, though she has the largest share (30 per cent) as compared with the U.S.A. (16·5 per cent) and West Germany (10 per cent). As the South African Minister for External Affairs remarked in 1962:

> The nations not supporting sanctions absorb 79·6 per cent of our exports and send us 63·7 per cent of our imports.

44. The Working Party rejects the view that the surest way of effecting liberal penetration is through the strengthening of South Africa's economy.[3] This view has been advanced for the last forty years, during which time the rights of Africans have been steadily reduced, not increased.

45. The facts concerning Britain's economic stake in South Africa are set out in Appendix XVI of the Report. The importance of this economic stake is a key factor in present British policy, and must be given weight in any consideration of the position: including a Christian one. To recognize this, however, does not justify giving practical en-

---

[1] Negotiations between the South Africa Government and the British Aircraft Corporation to supply the *Bloodhound* missile were placed in abeyance pending the General Election.

[2] Aircraft are now to be manufactured within South Africa. The first example is likely to be the French Fouga Magister or the Italian Macchi jet trainer, built under licence, and well suited for strafing ground targets undefended by anti-aircraft weapons. The latter 'plane is powered by British engines built under licence in Italy.

[3] See paras. 82–84, 89–91 of the Report.

couragement to *apartheid*. Some Africa states continue to import South African goods, as do Communist countries such as China, while small arms have been exported by Czechoslovakia.

46. Hitherto the attitude of the world community concerning South Africa has on all sides been more characterized by hot air and hypocrisy, than by effective action. The reason for this is the extraordinary difficulty of doing anything except by force to change the attitude of a government which is deaf to verbal protest from within and without, and in basic materials is self-supporting.[1]

B. *Policy of Sanctions*

47. To be effective, a policy of sanctions would amount to war against South Africa by the other members of the United Nations. The stages of this policy are seen by its supporters as follows:

Stage (*a*): The imposition of total sanctions, made effective by a naval blockade;[2]

Stage (*b*): Internal disorders provoked by the resulting economic distress;

Stage (*c*): The landing of a U.N. expeditionary force to prevent generalized chaos and massacre;

Stage (*d*): A conference under U.N. auspices to establish a new constitution with minority guarantees.

The justification for this policy is seen by its supporters in the doctrine of prophylactic violence. Hostilities of this kind could be limited, and controlled (by the West). The resultant bloodshed—believed in any case to be unavoidable—would be much less than it will otherwise be.

48. The case for and against this policy is considered in Section VIII of the Report. It must be recognized how tenuous in the present state of international law are the legal arguments for sanctions against South Africa because of her internal policies.[3] A fundamental consideration is that, though conceived in order to fight race war, this policy would in

---

[1] Oil represents only 13 per cent of South Africa's energy requirements. For an analysis of the oil question, see Appendix XVII of the Report, p. 144.

[2] Technical evidence shows that effective sanctions would require a naval blockade; that only total sanctions are a serious proposition; that South Africa could withstand such sanctions *by themselves* for a very long time. (Even in oil, South Africa could survive the total cessation of sea-borne imports for up to two years, and indefinitely if supplies were piped overland from Angola.) The whole concept of U.N. sanctions supposes Soviet agreement to suspend the cold war sufficiently for a major task force of American and British aircraft carriers to be withdrawn from their present assignments, for a period of years rather than months, in an operation which would be likely to be undertaken by the West primarily in order to prevent Communist domination of the tip of Africa.

[3] This point is examined in paras. 117–123 of the Report. The case of South-West Africa is very different (see paras. 136–142 of the Report and Appendix XIX, p. 150).

fact spark it off, since it is recognized that external blockade is likely to bring down the régime only if accompanied by internal insurrection. Yet as long as an open race war has not been provoked, it has not occurred; the time thus gained can still be used for a change of present *apartheid* policies by peaceful means. The peculiar danger of the South African situation lies in its 'open-endedness'. If a race war should break out there, there is no foretelling where it may end.

49. With regard to the argument of prophylactic violence, it must be observed that the conditions for a 'just war' against South Africa do not at present obtain.[1] Moreover, the Working Party, while deploring the violence already practised upon Africans, by legislation such as the Group Areas Act, are not prepared to support a policy which depends upon a calculation as to the relative merits of spilling x or y pints of human blood, anyway as long as there is any conceivable alternative.

c. *An Alternative Policy*

50. The Working Party does not accept the dilemma of either supporting coercion which could lead to war or of conniving at *apartheid*. Instead, it addressed itself to seeking an alternative course. We believe that realistic proposals must take account of existing British policy (wrong though we believe this to be); be related to the position within the Security Council; at each stage leave scope for a change in South African policies. This does not make the proposals themselves easy; they must be measured against the conflict in which South African racial policies could involve us all.

(i) *Explicit Dissociation from* Apartheid

51. This requires an analysis of those acts by Britain or her citizens which however tacitly encourage the Verwoerd Government in the pursuit of its present racial policy. This analysis is a matter which the Government should undertake, and propose remedies thereto to Parliament.

52. Such action would not by itself be, nor claim to be, coercive of South Africa. It would limit but not cut off trade between our two countries as would sanctions. Indeed, in some respects it would only apply further the logic of the U.K. vote in the Security Council (December 1963) prohibiting the export to South Africa of certain categories of strategic material. What it would do would be to make clear to South Africa and to the world our dissociation from a morally reprehensible policy, by discontinuing direct support for, and enjoyment of enhanced profits from, an economy which exploits racial oppression.

53. The kind of action envisaged by the Working Party is:

(*a*) To prohibit forthwith the supply of any further arms;

[1] Cp. para. 93 of the Report.

(*b*) to end all special privileges which remain from South Africa's former membership of the Commonwealth.

(*c*) To review the whole range of commercial relations with South Africa with a view to establishing those sectors where Britain could reasonably impose controls alone, and those where only collective action would make sense. Examples of action by Britain envisaged in the Report are the control of new capital investment and the imposition of surtax on repatriated South African dividends.[1]

(*d*) To discourage permanent emigration to South Africa.

It is needful for Britain, which has an investment in South Africa three times as great as that of the U.S.A., to consider the implications for ourselves of a remark made by a member of the South African Government:

So long as U.S. banks and business back us, we can go ahead.

54. Action in the commercial sector—such as the control of new capital investment in South Africa—would be painful. *But unless there is preparedness to take such limited steps, any discussion of sanctions must be ruled out of court.*

55. This policy of practical dissociation from *apartheid* would constitute a warning to South Africa to which she is fully entitled, since hitherto British action—as distinct from British words—has on the contrary encouraged South Africa to pursue her racial policies. An objection to the sanctions policy is that it would not be easy for a British Government to proceed from supplying Buccaneers to sending aircraft carriers as part of a U.N. sanction-enforcement unit; which the Buccaneers then sank. There would have to be intermediate stages. In this sense a policy of dissociation is a pre-requisite of a policy of sanctions. However, the former in no wise commits to adopting the latter subsequently, since it must be hoped that some change in South African policy may have occurred in the interval. The policy of dissociation from *apartheid* stands on its own merits. *The important point to establish is that it is the British Government's pressing responsibility to review the whole scope of this country's relations with South Africa, and to decide what peaceful measures are required to stop Britain or her citizens giving encouragement to* apartheid.

(ii) *Co-operation with the United Nations over South-West Africa*

56. Within the course of 1965, the International Court of Justice is to hand down its judgment in the case brought before it by Ethiopia and Liberia in 1960. The Court may declare that certain policies and legislation of an *apartheid* character in respect of South-West Africa are incompatible with South Africa's obligations under the mandate. If

[1] See paras. 165–175 of the Report.

South Africa refuses to amend these practices, the applicants are likely to seek redress from the Security Council under the provisions of the Charter.

57. At this juncture, Britain's full responsibility as a permanent member of the Security Council would be directly involved. The Working Party believes that Britain and the U.S.A. should together vote in favour of action by the Security Council to uphold the rule of law.

58. Such action could include a decision to impose economic sanctions. How this would differ from sanctions in respect of *apartheid* policies in South Africa as a whole is considered in Section IX of the Report. An essential point is that action would rest on the firm legal basis of a court judgment and a delict committed.

59. A condition of the 'just war' is the reasonable likelihood of the required objective being attained. *Provided* the Anglo-Saxon powers show real determination, it is unlikely that South Africa would decide to confront the world over South-West Africa, which is not the land of the Voortrekkers, and where her legal position is weak. Instead, she may seek to negotiate terms for withdrawal, of which the *sine qua non* would be the permanent demilitarization of the territory under international supervision. If such a withdrawal were to occur, the rule of law would have been shown to be effective, and this would be bound to be recognized in South Africa as well as the rest of the world.

60. The effects within South Africa of the two aspects of policy described under (i) and (ii) would be profound, for the U.K. and the U.S.A. would be seen to have made up their minds. Faced with a demand by the outside world for 'unconditional surrender', the South African whites would probably unite in one 'last ditch' laager.[1] Faced with clear but limited pressure—but only if so faced—there is still the possibility of South Africa deciding to change her course. It involves no less than undertaking to change the structure and way of life of South African society. For this, a calculation of self-interest is not enough: there must be a change of heart as well.

(iii) *Subsequent Perspectives*

61. These will depend not least on developments around South Africa. Immediately relevant in this context will be what happens in (*a*) Southern Rhodesia; (*b*) Mozambique and Angola, and (*c*) the High Commission Territories. Within South Africa, the first Bantustan in the Transkei is already showing some signs of developing a dynamic of its own.[2]

[1] Cp. paras. 105–7 of the Report.
[2] Though, as stressed in the Report, Africans will never accept the white-imposed Bantustans as adequate in their own land, and they are irrelevant to the basic issue of the urban labour force necessary if South Africa is to remain a modern industrial power.

62 It is fully recognized that the situation could worsen quickly, and events themselves outstrip the cautious approach of the Working Party. The Working Party believes that it will be necessary to keep the situation under close review, as changes in any of the surrounding territories could vitally affect a sound judgment of the South African situation. It commends this to the attention of the International Department.

63. The perspectives certainly do not justify any waiting upon events in relation to the policies outlined under (i) and (ii). If the British Government fails to grasp the nettle now, the peoples of South Africa and Britain will have to pay a heavy price later, when decisions far more difficult will have to be made.

64. It is against this background that we are obliged to consider the exercise of the Christian ministry of reconciliation. We have to recognize that the normal time required for the kind of social revolution that is necessary in South Africa is no longer available in international terms. We are thus obliged at one and the same time to apply a measure of external pressure and to do all that is possible to develop dialogue and fellowship with South African Christians. Pressure can only be a function of the state, yet many Christians in Britain would associate themselves with that pressure. Dialogue is the opportunity of the Church, yet the dialogue has to be conducted in the atmosphere created by the pressure, and not by trying to forget it.

IV. ACTION BY THE BRITISH CHURCHES

A. *Inter-Church Relations*

65. It must be squarely faced that the numerous resolutions adopted by Churches and Councils of Churches throughout the world condemning *apartheid* during the past fifteen years have had little positive effect in changing the attitudes of the Churches in South Africa.

66. We must say *the* Churches in South Africa, for although the Churches, which are members of the Christian Council of South Africa have condemned separate development—have, for instance, held large public meetings to protest against the renewal of the 90-day Clause, unheeded by the Government—they nevertheless often practise it in their own church lives. (The physical fact of separate development is, of course, responsible for much of this.) More particularly, a majority of the English-speaking population, which provides the white membership of the Christian Council Churches, now tacitly supports separate development, and, like the United Party[1] which is its chief political expression, has no alternative policy to offer.

---

[1] Officially, the United Party's policy is 'a race federation plan that would maintain Western standards and give non-whites an immediate participation and sense of function in government'.

67. More important than these Churches in terms of relationships with the Government are the three Dutch Reformed Churches. Of these, the largest, oldest and most realistic, the Nederduits Gereformeerde Kerk, has made discreet démarches to the Government protesting against particular injustices in *apartheid* legislation, and has persuaded the Government to change certain of them. But basically the N.G. Church approves of separate development, not on scriptural grounds, but on grounds of political, economic and social expediency. In the practice of parallel congregations they see the early-begun implementation of the oft-repeated recommendation of international missionary conferences to indigenize the African Church. The Gereformeerde and Hervormde Churches are much smaller;[1] the latter contains many who would still justify *apartheid* on their own reading of Old Testament scripture.

68. Between these Churches and member Churches of the World Council of Churches communication on the race issue has largely broken down following the Cottesloe conference in which they participated in December 1960. Yet without fellowship and genuine interchange of biblical scholarship, the possibility of dialogue is slim. The position has now been reached where there can be no direct official discussion with representatives of the Dutch Reformed Churches concerning the race issue. To re-establish the conditions for fruitful dialogue, we and they together need to realize afresh our common faith and obedience to the Gospel. It is as though we had to meet a stranger Church and begin with those things which unite us. Thereafter it may be possible for us to express with due humility and understanding our concern for inter-racial fellowship and for this to find a hearing.

69. A meeting with the Dutch Reformed Churches is most possible within the family of the Reformed Churches. The Working Party therefore welcomed the news that, following the visit of its Chairman and Secretary to South Africa, proposals are at present being considered for an invitation to this country of certain ministers of those Churches. These visits are planned to take place next year, if approved by the Committees of the Churches concerned in Great Britain and South Africa. It is hoped they will be followed by other visits in succeeding years, and by return visits. The Working Party is certain that the International Department and the British Council of Churches will wish to encourage this initiative, which will include both African and white Christians from the Presbyterian Church of South Africa as well as from the Dutch Reformed Churches.

70. Parallel with these invitations from the Presbyterian Churches in this island, the Working Party hopes the International Department

---

[1] For full church statistics, see Appendix IV of the Report, p. 102. See also Section IV of the Report.

will encourage invitations from other member Churches of the British
Council of Churches to ministers and laymen of all races of the Churches
which are members of the Christian Council of South Africa and,
through the Inter-Denominational African Ministers' Federation, of
Independent (separatist) Churches; and return visits. The chief difficulty is finance, because of the expense of travel to and from South
Africa. The Working Party believes that trust funds should be
approached in this connection, and that this whole initiative should be
given high priority. It is here that the Churches can make a more practical contribution than by passing yet more resolutions, which often have
the opposite effect in South Africa, while creating the feeling among
Christians in this country that something has been 'done' and conscience
is discharged from further action.

71. At the same time as we undertake this new approach, we need
the clarity of vision to see that we cannot, though potential hosts seeking
ways and means of greater understanding, refrain from making clear
the principles we believe to be at stake in the confrontation of the white
and black races in the world, and in particular in South Africa.

B. *Relief for the Families of Political Prisoners and of 90-day Clause*
Detainees

72. This is the second sphere where the Churches can do something
practical; as, indeed, they have been doing, in particular through
Christian Aid.

73. At its thirty-sixth meeting, in April 1960, the British Council of
Churches adopted the following resolution:

> The Council commends to the generosity of the members of its
> constituent Churches the plight of those at present suffering in
> South Africa through the policy of *apartheid*. The Council is glad
> that the Division of Inter-Church Aid and Service to Refugees of
> the World Council of Churches has already made resources avail-
> able to meet this need, and offers its own Department of Inter-
> Church Aid and Refugee Service to receive gifts for this purpose.
> The Council further commends the Defence and Aid Fund of
> Christian Action as a channel of Christian generosity.

74. The present facts are set out in Appendix XVIII to the Report.

75. In 1964-65 there are three different needs. These are:

(a) Aid for legal defence of those charged under *apartheid* legislation;

(b) Relief for the dependants of political prisoners under trial or
sentence, as well as of those detained without trial under the 90-
day Clause;

(*c*) Aid for refugees.

Each case requires careful individual investigation.

76. With regard to (*b*) and (*c*), the proper channel in this country is the Christian Aid Department of the British Council of Churches. The World Council of Churches Division of Inter-Church Aid, Refugee and World Service has recently appealed to its related agencies (i.e. Christian Aid in the British Isles) for $1,000,000 for current emergencies in Africa, which includes substantial aid for South African refugees and for the dependants of prisoners and detainees. Christian Aid has sent a first contibution of £20,000. The member Churches should give all possible support to Christian Aid for the African appeal. In addition, funds received by Christian Aid designated for (*a*), for which there is also pressing need, will be passed on to the appropriate organization.

77. In view of the criticisms which have been made in some South African circles, it is important to note that such giving in no wise fails to recognize the right of a government to restrain disruptive forces. But a government which imposes inequality such as exists in South Africa, and then denies so many of its citizens any constitutional method of protest or redress, is itself responsible for creating forces of disruption,[1] which are then entitled to outside sympathy and human assistance. Beyond this, however, Christians have a special obligation to those who suffer when innocent of any illegality: the many who would have been condemned but for the provision of legal defence, and the wives and children of those who are on remand, on trial, sentenced (including some executed), banned, or detained under the 90-day Clause.

c. *Intercession*

78. There can be a danger in circumstances of moral indignation that prayer *for* may take on the overtones of prayer *against*. At best, it involves a sense of distinction from those for whom we are praying. In intercession for South Africa, the call comes to Christians in this country to pray *with* Christians in South Africa, of whom many are seeking God's help and guidance in being faithful to Jesus Christ in a situation of great complexity, difficulty and often personal danger and suffering.

79. A great enemy in South Africa is fear. The tragedy of this may be judged from the following passage from a letter written by an African priest to the Secretary of the Working Party on 17th June 1964:

> Changes are bound to come about sooner or later. About that there is no shadow of doubt. We have no choice at all in the matter. The question is, will these changes come about as a result of violence and counter-violence and more violence? Unless there is a radical

[1] Cp. Appendix IX of the Report, para. 14, p. 122.

change of heart and will on the part of the black and white, the future
is very dark indeed and threatening. As you know, the white man's
policy is based on fear. I sometimes try to stand in his shoes. I con-
fess he has reason to fear. I would too, I suppose, if I were white.
What saddens me is that I cannot get near enough to him to enable
him to see and know me, and also to assure him that I honestly will
not do him any harm. Moreover, I want to take immediate steps
together with him to ensure a happy future for both of us. We must
work for the future together, and not, as it is at present, entirely
on his own terms. Time is not on his side, nor on mine, and if he
is unwilling to meet me and talk, so much worse for both of us. Here,
then, is my dilemma. If only I could come closer to him I might yet
rid him of his fear, which paralyses him and me.

80. Such yearnings and fears, together with the suffering caused by
selfishness, blindness and lack of imagination, we may take with us into
the light which surrounds God's throne, as we kneel in our daily ministry of intercession. This is the continuing responsibility of Christians
in Britain as instruments of God's purpose and fellow-workers with
Him in the working out of His love for all who live in South Africa.

V. CONCLUSION

81. It has been said that for the historian the only rule is to recognize
the play of the contingent and the unforeseen.[1] The insight of the Christian faith descries, not the contingent and the unforeseen, but that we
see only the reverse side of the pattern God is weaving for the reconciliation of the world He made. What is unforeseen—continually surprising and humbling—is the wonderful resource of God's love, which, un-
resting and unhasting, turns even the wrath of man to His praise. A
blasphemy the Christian can never commit is to say that any human
situation has passed the point of no return, has entered a realm where
hope, faith, mercy and reconciliation no longer operate, with a potency
limited only by our own lack of belief. For this reason the dark situation
in South Africa is yet full of hope, because we know that God is indeed
able to transform the outcome of our attempted obedience. South
Africa has not passed outside the saving act of God in Jesus Christ. The
calling of Christians is to be faithful to Him.

[1] H. A. L. Fisher, in the preface to *A History of Europe.*

Note to page 18

In November the Labour Government decided to embargo new arms contracts,
but to authorize the delivery of the 16 Buccaneer aircraft in 1965, and spare
parts thereafter to maintain them. These aircraft constituted almost the totality
of outstanding arms deliveries. The reason given was respect of existing contracts (advance payments had been made).

4

REPORT

I. TERMS OF REFERENCE

1. The British Council of Churches, at its meeting in Bristol on 16th October 1963, instructed its International Department 'to give further study to the problems connected with the future of South Africa and all her people. In particular this study should include the issue of *sanctions* and the question of *South-West Africa*.'[1]

2. We have regarded this report as having two purposes: information and action.

Information

To set out the present position in South Africa as objectively as possible, in particular the issue of *apartheid*, or separate development, in terms of:

(1) Its meaning for the lives of individual citizens;

(2) Its effect on the witness of the Church;

(3) The effect of the Churches' attitude towards it on their possibilities for witness now and in the future, particularly in Africa.

Action

Here there are two requirements: the first concerns the action of the Church in relation to the state; the second, the action of the Church within its own sphere of executive competence.

A. (i) To help individual Christians in the United Kingdom to enter into the dimensions of a problem which must be a subject for their prayer, and on which as citizens they are required to pass political judgment.

A. (ii) To guide the British Council of Churches in its corporate responsibility in relation to the international policy of the United Kingdom Government.

B. To enable the British Council of Churches to decide what action it can take within the fellowship of the world-wide Church.

3. Underlying all our discussions there has been the consciousness of the gravity of the situation we have been studying, a situation we be-

[1] For membership of the Working Party, and its programme of meetings, see Appendices I and II, pp. 97-100.

lieve to be deteriorating in its international context and becoming increasingly explosive within South Africa.

4. A fundamental difficulty, which the reader should bear in mind throughout the Report, is how far it is not only permitted, but required of us, to press for grave action now, in order to prevent having to face a yet graver situation in the future, when prophylactic action will no longer be possible. The answer in no case can be that the end can justify the means. Any course of action proposed, therefore, must spring—and be seen to spring—from Christian compassion and love, of which true justice is an integral part.

II. THE RESPONSIBILITY OF THE BRITISH COUNCIL OF CHURCHES IN CALLING FOR THIS STUDY

5. We know that the Council was aware of a heavy responsibility when it asked for this study to be undertaken. In private life we can only enter a neighbour's house by due process of law, however much we may be aware of internal disharmony there; we can only act in the same way between nations. We are, however, members of one Catholic Church and citizens of one world. If, therefore, God gives to any of us a word of prophecy, this cannot be restricted to our own borders. Wherever there is discord among peoples our faith calls us to seek to create harmony, through contributing to mercy and justice among men.

6. This is true of the Church in any country. There is a further measure of responsibility which lies particularly on Christians in the United Kingdom; it stems from Britain's historic connection with South Africa, and from both the sound policies and the mistaken ones she has exercised there.

7. Britain, however, has historic connections with many parts of the world. There are also many parts of the world where fundamental human rights are violated.[1] Why then should special attention be paid to South Africa? The answer is that three factors justify special concern. First, a system which deliberately breaks up family life is erected into a principle, and given legislative enactment. Secondly, the system cannot be divorced from the assumption and practice by many white South Africans of domination and exploitation of one race by another, reflecting a view degrading to man as made in the image of God. Thirdly, the resultant situation could within this decade lead to a world conflict in which the inhabitants of the United Kingdom would be involved.

8. The need to understand the issues involved, though at a distance, is, therefore, imperative. In the first place, that if the way opens for the Church in any part of the world to act in mediation, our thinking may

[1] Though nowhere else is this done so explicitly on the basis of a quality over which a man has no control: the colour of his skin.

be prepared. In the second, that our intercession may enter into the real dimensions of the situation. In the third, that Christian opinion may be crystallized and have some influence on our Government when they make their decisions concerning South Africa.

9. Moreover, there are related questions facing citizens of the United Kingdom to which they have to give answers; questions such as the well-being of the High Commission Territories and the attitude we should take concerning South-West Africa. This latter could prove the focal point of an international crisis within a year.

III. THE SPIRIT OF THIS ENQUIRY

10. In this study we have need to be humble. We have been reminded that 'it is difficult for people in Britain to speak when they do not have to bear the cross of reconciliation'. We must needs keep in mind failures in tolerance and justice within the life of our own country, in the spirit of Mrs Pandit who, when speaking for India during the Security Council debate on South Africa, in August 1963, said:

> We are conscious of our shortcomings, our failures. We are in no position to condemn. But, like other sister nations, we believe that there is a moral law which must be recognized and obeyed if mankind is to continue its onward march towards a brave new world. Because of this belief, our Government seeks to implement the promise of justice and equality enshrined in all democratic constitutions into the life of every citizen. The pace may sometimes be slower than we would wish, but nevertheless we move on and strive for the elimination of discrimination and the breaking down of all artificial barriers which separate men from each other.

11. At the outset we have tried to face our own ignorance and our liability to bias in any attempt to understand the views of the different sections of the South African community. We have reminded ourselves that we are members of a comparatively stable society in which changes of balance between different groups have for many years been achieved without violence. Our national history, it is true, reveals instances of grave group injustice; but these have in large part been righted through gradual change, though not without harsh legal control of protesters in the process. Today, one of us may be descended both from a Tolpuddle martyr and one of the Dorset magistrates who sentenced him. What is equally important in the present context is that we have as our ecclesiastical ancestors both the local preacher who claimed the right of agricultural workers to associate, and the churchwarden who regarded this as a threat to law and order calling for the exercise of the 37th article of religion. We have not experienced a situation in which increasing pressures from an unrepresented majority do not begin to win a

response within the body politic. We have not experienced the despera-
tion of those who believe that violent resistance is all that is left to them,
and who challenge us to explain the ethical difference between resisting
by force sustained threats to personal liberty when they come from inside the state, and when they come from outside.

12. On the other hand, the gradualness of our own social revolution
has saved us from experiencing the bitter deprivations that have come
to the privileged classes in some of the violent revolutions of this century. We do not therefore appreciate what it means to be faced with the
challenge to make concessions which appear to us to mean the giving
up of a position of privilege, and appear to many white South Africans
to mean losing their way of life, or even their homeland.

13. Again, we have never, unless maybe we were in a Japanese pri-
soner-of-war camp or in parts of the Congo in the autumn of 1960,
begun to understand what it is to suffer indignity because of the colour
of our skin. A searching statement of this experience is that of Dr
Luther King, part of whose letter from prison is reproduced in Appendix III.

IV. THE FELLOWSHIP OF THE CHURCH

14. A prerequisite to study and action is close and prayerful contact
with the Church in South Africa. There are five main groups we need
to consider:

(i) The Dutch Reformed Churches (Nederduits Gereformeerde
Kerk, Nederduits Hervormde Kerk, Gereformeerde Kerk),
comprising 24 per cent of the Christians of the country (for
fuller statistics see Appendix IV).

(ii) The member Churches of the Christian Council of South Africa
(Church of the Province, Methodist, Lutheran, Presbyterian,
Congregational, Baptist, Reformed, Salvation Army and twenty
smaller Churches), 45 per cent;

(iii) The Roman Catholic Church, 7 per cent;

(iv) The Independent Bantu Churches, sometimes called separatist
or sect Churches, 18 per cent;

(v) The Pentecostal and other Churches, 6 per cent.

15. There is yet another, and smaller, group: those, mainly African
men, who are seeking against difficult odds to maintain a personal relationship with Christ outside the fellowship of the visible Church, because they feel deeply that the Church, by what it has done and what it
has left undone, has betrayed the integrity of non-whites as persons, and
thereby left unfulfilled our Lord's command to love our neighbours as
ourselves.

16. Our most direct contact is with the second of these groups, which forms a fellow Council with the British Council of Churches in the World Council of Churches. Many of these Churches have their origin in Britain, and some of them still have definite links of mutual service, particularly within the ministry.

17. The leaders of the Christian Council are aware, however, that the Council itself and its committees do not yet adequately reflect the spread of its membership, and they are seeking to achieve more active non-white participation. Even when fellowship is real, the inhibiting effect of the lack of spontaneous social contact is not always recognized. Those who have lived through the change from colonial rule to independence, not only in Africa, bear witness to the release this brings in freedom of expression in what have already been quite intimate relationships. The European has honestly thought that hitherto there was uninhibited discussion among equals; but he faced a new revelation when his non-European colleague suddenly knew that he was speaking from a position of equality, not only personally in himself but corporately in his people.

18. A necessary point of contact with African Christian thought in this situation is fortunately afforded by the Inter-Denominational African Ministers' Federation. The Federation has a wider membership than the Christian Council, including on one side African ministers of the Dutch Reformed Missionary Churches, and on the other ministers of some of the Independent Bantu Churches.

19. During a mission to South Africa, the Chairman and Secretary of the Working Party had friendly contact with the Secretaries of the Christian Council, the I.D.A.M. Federation and the Christian Institute of Southern Africa, and with leaders of the Dutch Reformed and Roman Catholic Churches.

20. There are then a number of strands which can be gathered to weave deeper fellowship between the Churches of Britain and South Africa. As much use as possible has been made of these in preparing this report.

21. The need to enlarge and deepen Christian understanding and fellowship between our Churches and those in South Africa is so great that the Working Party believes special measures are called for.

22. Neither we nor the Church in South Africa can forget that this fellowship involves Churches in other parts of Africa. What the Church in South Africa has already contributed to the All Africa Conference of Churches, not least in providing it with its first General Secretary in the person of Dr D. G. S. M'Timkulu, is a token of this. There is a debit side as well. Some of the Churches in West Africa face setbacks in their mission because of racial discrimination in South Africa. Christians in Nigeria and Sierra Leone have been challenged by Muslims about

c

the validity of their faith on this account. It was Dr Ben Marais of the Dutch Reformed Church, writing from within South Africa in 1958 on the subject 'Cross or Crescent in Africa', who said:

> Christianity is making great strides. Its greatest problem, however, is as yet unsolved: how to create real deep community among different racial groups. If Christianity ultimately fails in this it must fail to win the heart of Africa. For whether Christianity or Islam will be victorious in Africa may well depend on the solution of this problem.

23. Much the same has to be said of the challenge of Communistic atheism in Africa. It was of French-speaking West Africa that it was said: 'The left wing has won the trust of Africans by behaving in ways that Africans had never seen Europeans behave; they were personal friends and comrades, rather than Europeans.' From similar experience of day-by-day friendship Chief Luthuli, when accused of being a Communist, answered:

> Now, we don't know Communism; all we know is that these men and women came to us to help us. I don't deny that some might have ulterior motives; all I am concerned about is that they came to assist us in fighting racial oppression; and they have no trace of racialism or of being patronizing—just no trace of it at all.

Within the fellowship of the Church there must come a deeper penitence among white Christians in every continent when the harsh truth is faced that Communists and humanists may go into the Kingdom before us, because they 'did it unto one of these little ones' and we 'did it not'.

V. THE PRESENT POSITION IN SOUTH AFRICA

24. The population of the Republic of South Africa today is approximately 17 million,[1] divided as follows:

Whites	$3\frac{1}{2}$ million[2]
Coloureds	$1\frac{1}{2}$ million[3]
Asians	$\frac{1}{2}$ million[4]
Africans	$11\frac{1}{2}$ million[5]

[1] Cp. also Appendix IV, p. 102.
[2] Afrikaans-speaking: 2 million; English-speaking: $1\frac{1}{2}$ million.
[3] Descendants of mixed race from Hottentots, imported slaves from East and West Africa and Madagascar, and Europeans.
[4] Descendants of Indian indentured labourers on Natal sugar plantations, their original homes being in both India and Pakistan.
[5] Figures from the 1951 census for the relative numerical strength of the African tribes were as follows (hence are posed serious language, and therefor educational, problems):

Xhosa	3,400,000	Tswana	860,000
Zulu	2,900,000	Venda and	
Sotho	2,200,000	others	1,350,000

The total population increased between 1951 and 1960 by 25 per cent, the group increases being: White, 16 per cent; coloured, 35 per cent; Asian, 30 per cent and African, 26 per cent.

25. These seventeen million people live in a country of approximately 475,000 square miles, of which some 65,000 square miles (or 13 per cent)[1] comprise the land set aside for African occupation, previously known as 'Native Reserves', and now as 'Bantu Homelands'. Of the 11½ million Africans, some 4 million live in these areas, while the rest live in 'white' areas, 4 million in towns and 3½ million on European farms.

26. The relevant point is the two irreversible trends in the population. These are:

(i) With every year that passes, non-whites represent a greater proportion of the total population.

(ii) In spite of influx control, a greater and greater number of Africans are becoming part of the voteless urban proletariat.

In his new book, *The Two Faces of Africa*,[2] Professor Marais describes these trends as follows:

> In 1920 approximately 14 per cent of the non-white population of South Africa lived in the white urban areas. In 1940 this percentage had risen by 6 per cent. But by 1950 it had risen by another 8 per cent to 28 per cent and by 1960—after twelve years of *apartheid*—it had risen to 37 per cent. If this trend continues and in spite of all measures taken there is little indication that it can or will be arrested: it will be 42 per cent in 1970 and 70 per cent in 1990. These figures, to be fully grasped, must be seen against the background of population increase in South Africa. The 20 per cent of 1940 was 20 per cent of nine million: the 37 per cent of 1960 amounted to 37 per cent of about 12 millions. By 1990 it will be 70 per cent of 23 million non-whites. By that date we should, in the light of present trends, have 5 million whites in South Africa. This makes nonsense of *apartheid* or separate development.

The most recent census figures show Professor Marais' estimate to have been too conservative, as they reveal that *between 1951 and 1960, the African urban population actually increased by more than 1 million (over 40 per cent).* Even therefore if the Bantustan policy were to succeed in the Transkei, it would not touch the real problem: the 60 per cent of all the Africans who live in white areas. After fifteen years of *apartheid* policy the great black stream to the white cities continues. Nor can it be otherwise, for the whole South African economy depends

---

[1] A proportion of the 'white' 87 per cent is desert.
[2] Shuter and Shooter, Pietermaritzburg, 1964, p. 45.

on their labour.[1] The policy of separate development therefore means the separation of a minority in Bantustans, and discrimination against the segregated majority who no longer live there. It is for this reason that the Bantustan policy has been referred to in South Africa as 'The Pursuit of the Irrelevant'.[2]

27. When the Union of South Africa was constituted in 1910 there were two conflicting policies in being regarding the rights of non-whites. In the former South African Republic, now the Transvaal, the constitution had stated categorically that 'the people desire to permit no equality[3] between coloured people and the white inhabitants of the country, either in Church or state'. The same view prevailed in the other Boer Republic, the Orange Free State. In the old Cape Colony, on the other hand, there was a franchise based on property and education, not colour; while Natal policy was similar in theory, though not in practice. In everyday affairs these policies may not always have produced much difference in social practice, but the Cape franchise reflected a radically different view of race relations.

28. The United Kingdom Government had to choose between forming the Union in 1910 and a standing on the principle of the Cape franchise for the whole country. It chose the former, hoping that the more liberal policy would prevail. This hope has not been fulfilled; on the contrary, in 1936 Cape Africans were placed on a separate roll for the election of three white Members of Parliament, and even this modified franchise was abolished in 1959. The policy of the new Republic is thus the fulfilment of that of the old Republic across sixty years: apart from the Reserves, the 'Bantu homelands'. South Africa is a white man's country in which only white people have the right to full citizenship. No others, whether Coloured, Asian or African, however many generations old in the area in which they are living, whatever their educational, property or other qualifications, can enjoy normal civic rights. By law,

---

[1] For instance, according to figures published by the South African Bureau of Statistics, five major employment divisions—mining, manufacturing, construction, the railways and the post office—employed nearly three times as many non-whites as whites. The total number employed in these five divisions in April 1963 was 1,729,000, of which only 458,000 were whites.

[2] When we come to consider possible alternative policies—as we do in the next Section—it is worth noting the comment which these facts concerning the Bantustan policy inspired in the *Rand Daily Mail*:

> South Africa's failure is that we have to choose between integration and separation of races, but we cannot bring ourselves to face the logical consequences of either course. This is a dilemma of unacceptable alternatives. As a nation we have lost our way because we are afraid to follow the logical path in either direction. What we are trying to do is to enjoy the benefit of economic integration while refusing the discomforts of social and political integration.

Many of the white population have not yet accepted that they cannot have the labour of millions of Africans *without having them as well*.

[3] *Gelijkstelling*—'putting on an equality'.

they must live in socially, and in a number of respects economically, segregated communities.

29. The stated aim of the present form of this policy, now called 'separate development', is to provide the appropriate physical and mental environment for the separate development of all ethnic groups in the country: white, Coloured, Asian, Xhosa, Zulu, Sotho, Tswana, Venda. The heart of the policy for Africans, but not for Coloureds and Asians, is the constituting of separate semi-self-governing territories in the traditional areas associated with the main tribal groups.[1]

30. The Transkei, home of the Xhosas, the first Bantustan to be inaugurated, held its first elections in November 1963. Of the Legislative Assembly, 45 are elected and 64 nominated, the latter being the government-appointed chiefs.[2] Voting is by those Xhosas who are qualified, whether resident in the Transkei or elsewhere in South Africa. The Transkei Constitution excludes the following matters from the competence of the Assembly: defence; foreign affairs; customs and excise; immigration; currency; banks and loans; railways, airports and harbours; the South African courts and police; broadcasting; post, telegraphs and telephones. Disallowance of bills lies with the President of the Republic. The Constitution itself can be suspended by the South African Government, with due notice. There is no representation of the Territory and its inhabitants in the Parliament of the Republic, which remains a white-only body, and continues to legislate for the Territory on all essential matters. That there is no question of genuine self-government was stressed by the Prime Minister, Dr Verwoerd, in the Senate on 1st May 1961.

31. Much planning and devoted personal service has been given in recent years to the development of the Transkei, as indeed to the other Reserves, in, for instance, health and education. The Government is seeking to create economically viable territories which will absorb the Africans who are forced back from the white areas into permanent residence. More than £500,000 has already been loaned to help African businessmen there. This, however, is a small sum compared with the millions invested in developing the 'border' industries set up, not in the natural demographic centres of the Transkei, but just over the border in 'white' South Africa, within daily travelling of African homes. These 'border' industries are in a monoply position vis-à-vis African labour, and are able to exploit the absence of alternative employment to keep

---

[1] The revealing maps of the Tomlinson Report show that only in the case of the Transkei does an African reserve really form a geographic unity. The other 260 African reserves are spread all over South Africa. In the Transvaal alone, there are eighty-four African areas. They cannot therefore become Bantustans on the Transkeian pattern.
[2] This is not to suggest the political situation in the Transkei is settled. Several chiefs have supported the Opposition.

wages down. Indeed, cheap labour has been offered to British firms as an inducement to set up factories in these areas (Cyril Lord is an example). Whereas the Tomlinson Report in 1954 recommended that £110,000,000 be spent on the Bantustans over the ensuing ten years, in the first nine only £3,500,000 has been spent. One reason for this is that it is not government policy for any industry to be set up within a Bantustan until such time as African capital and African managerial skills are available to develop it.

32. What has been done is, moreover, effective only in one area: the Transkei. For the other areas it is so far paper planning. This explains the strength of the language used by *The Times* in a leading article on 8th May 1964 following the passing of the Bantu Laws Amendment Bill.

Apart from the unanswerable objection that the seven million Africans in white South Africa can never possibly be accommodated, employed or fed in these so-called 'homelands', it is typical of the practice of *apartheid* that their rights in white South Africa are extinguished before the homelands are made ready for them. So far there is only the Transkei, nominally governed by Africans, but still without the complex of border industries which, so it is said, will make it a magnet to all Xhosa nationals outside. The other reserves are still reserves, overpopulated and undeveloped.

33. It is needful to stress the conflict between the border industries and the principle of territorial separation. Instead of drawing back African workers from the white cities, they are likely to draw more and more rural Africans into these new industrial areas. To draw back millions of Africans at present living in the white areas to the homelands would require the fulfilment of two conditions:

(1) the creation of an industrial machine which can compete with the labour demand of the existing industries in the white cities; this would require decades and an immense imput of white capital (leading to increased competition with existing white industry);

(2) a major redistribution of white land to the Bantustans, to carry and feed the millions who would come to live there.[1]

Neither of these conditions are to be fulfilled, capital investment for the reason given in the preceding paragraph, and land redistribution because of the attitude of the white electorate. In a speech in Durban on 27th August 1963, Dr Verwoerd said in this connection:

[1] The Reserves already carry 63 persons per square mile, whereas the rest of South Africa carries only 27 persons per square mile in spite of heavy industrial development.

The government is only prepared to give to each group what history has given it.

34. For the many millions of non-whites living and working in 'white' South Africa, new townships and accompanying services have been created, involving an investment of more than £100,000,000 during the past ten years. These, though regimented in lay-out, provide better accommodation and minimal communal facilities than in most of the areas they replace. They have, however, removed workers much further from their place of work, and have eliminated freehold rights where they existed, thus removing security and a sense of belonging. There is also closer surveillance by the authorities of the inhabitants and their activities. In the largest of the towns lines of demaraction are laid down between quarters for different African tribal groups. Local government responsibility is being increasingly given to the inhabitants within the limits of the townships, but they are regarded as temporary migrants with a work permit, whose real home is in a Bantustan.[1] Thus although in the Johannesburg area, for example, there are 711,000 Africans and 389,690 whites, the former do not enjoy any civic or social rights outside the suburb in which they live; their journey to and from the city centre is for the purpose of working[2] for the white community in industry, or domestic service, or making their purchases in the better shopping facilities of the city.

35. For Asians, many of whom are traders and certainly not farmers, the policy holds out only the pattern of segregation with minimal local government rights. This is resulting in displacement to new townships on the periphery of white urban centres with an extremely disintegrating effect on economic life—sometimes to the extent of economic ruin— since their previous more centrally situated stores were patronized by all sections of the community.[3] For the 1½ million Coloureds, for whom again there is no Bantustan, there is only the prospect of second-class citizenship for themselves and their children; a citizenship of decreas-

[1] This explains why the Conference of Roman Catholic Bishops of South Africa declared on 17th March 1964 that the Bantu Law Amendment Act 'strips the African of his basic freedoms in the country of his birth, making him dependent upon the possession of a permit to explain his presence anywhere, and at any time, outside the "Bantu homelands". This is not consonant with any concept of the dignity of the human person.'

[2] Unemployment among the African labour force in Soweto is not high. Of the 232,904 males registered by the Non-European Affairs Dept. of the City of Johannesburg on 31st March 1964, 11,602 were unemployed—or only 4·9 per cent Juvenile unemployment (16–19 years) was as low as 2·9 per cent.

[3] The same result is sometimes achieved by deliberate white boycott of purchases. In many Transvaal towns Afrikaans-speaking citizens have used boycotts to force out Indian traders. Examples of this have occurred in towns such as Rustenberg, Standerton, Bethal and Ermelo. *The Guardian*, 22nd April 1964.

ing value, with every new addition of traditional Coloured jobs to the list of those reserved for white persons.

36. This job reservation resulting from the Civilized Labour Policy[1] dates from the early 1920s. The Afrikaners had once been a nation of farmers, but increased population and reduction in the size of holdings led to an influx of 'poor whites' to the towns. This lay on the conscience of the community, and was met by legal action to enforce and extend a convention that might otherwise have wasted away. Employment in certain categories in certain industries was reserved for whites; the list has been steadily increased, even though whites have not always been available and in spite of the views of the industrialists.

37. Separate development is applied to the whole of education[2] including that at university level. There are now separate university colleges for the main African groups. The old University College of Fort Hare is now limited to Xhosas. Non-white undergraduates are not allowed to enrol in any white university. It is difficult to assess the total loss to all communities through the resulting lack of a meeting of minds at the student level.

38. Separate development, with its movement of peoples, has been effected by government decision, that is, white decision. It has, it is true, provided better housing for thousands of families. In many ways it has done so in a framework not very dissimilar from that which would have resulted from natural economic and social forces; left to themselves no doubt, most Zulus would have chosen to live in a mainly Zulu suburb. Similarly African teachers would have made changes in the school curriculum which reflected their own culture. This has already happened in the music and literature of Johannesburg, where freely developing growth has produced art forms which are neither traditional Bantu nor traditional European, but something new, enriched by a double heritage. What has been done by Government, however, has been without consultation with the people concerned and without their free consent; for they do not exist as political entities.

39. The separate development policy is thus neither creating viable economic territories in the reserves, nor solving the problem of residence with normal human rights within 'white' South Africa for the millions of Africans, Coloureds and Asians who are living and working there and have nowhere else to go. *Seven and a half million Africans, who cannot possibly be accommodated in the Bantustans, are now by law temporary residents without family rights, in four-fifths of the Republic.* An African may only remain in an urban area if he possesses a work-seeker's permit. If he becomes unemployed for any reason, whether through retrench-

---

[1] See Appendix V, p. 103.
[2] For an assessment of the effect of the Bantu Education Act, see Appendix VI, p. 105. This is such an important matter that it requires separate treatment.

ment, dismissal or illness, and fails to report at the labour bureau within seventy-two hours, he is 'endorsed out' of the area, even if he has lived there all his life and his children are growing up in school there; if, having reported, he fails to obtain a new job within a month, he must by law be 'endorsed out'. This means that he must go back to his traditional homeland, already over-crowded, even though he has personally had no contact for years, or ever, with any village there. Now that the Bantu Affairs Act has become law, the sole test of whether an African can remain in an urban area is the need for his labour, as determined by the State Labour Bureau.[1]

40. Not only civic rights and freedom of movement are denied to the urban African; family rights are legally denied and families broken up.[2] This strikes at the root of Christian teaching concerning the home. A man, even though temporarily permitted to work in a town, has no right to have his wife and family with him except under increasingly stringent conditions. Without his wife he is forced to live in so-called 'bachelor' quarters. In Langa Township, Cape Town (1960), out of a population of 25,000, 17,000 were 'bachelors'. The social and moral problems implicit in this situation are evident.

41. To maintain this policy the urban African is subject to police action which, in theory and not merely in practice, denies human liberty and fundamental human rights. In the last ten years the average number of black South Africans convicted each year of violating supervision and control regulations has been 370,000, or just over 1,000 *a day*. The adverse effect on parental control of children through the non-return of father or mother after the day's work because they were picked up for a pass offence, by itself comprises a most serious indictment of the system. Moreover, people feel that what the police are doing is unjust, and they see their friends or themselves put in prison for actions they do not regard as anti-social. This brings the whole of the law into disregard, contributing directly to the development of *tsotsis*, the violent 'teddy-boys' of the African townships. The police have been given powers that no one should be allowed to have over his fellows, such as the right of entry without warrant to private premises at all times, and

---

[1] For details of the most recent legislation, see Appendix VII, p. 114.

[2] A case which occurred in the household of a member of a Congregational Church in Cape Town, of which the Secretary of the Working Party learned when there in May 1964, was the following. The African maid married. To prevent her raising a family in Cape Town, she was 'endorsed out' on the grounds she had been resident west of the 'Eiselen line' for only nine years and not ten. As she had nowhere else to go, she was forcibly put on the train to Kimberley, where her only connection was that, many years before, she had nursed a sick uncle there who had long since died. She had no relations in Kimberley, no home to go to, no job. Her marriage, one month old, was subjected to indefinite separation from her husband, who will lose his job if he leaves Cape Town to rejoin his wife.

the power of indefinite committal to prison on suspicion, without trial, under the 90-day Clause.

42. The increasing unrest of non-whites under these restrictions has brought more oppression by way of legislation. Under the General Law Amendment Act of 1964, the Minister of Justice has power to detain for indefinite periods anyone convicted of certain political offences, and also the right to detain anyone incommunicado for interrogation for renewable periods of ninety days until such time as he has, in the opinion of the Commissioner of Police, replied satisfactorily to all questions.[1] In 1963, 3,350 persons were detained under the various security laws.

43. It would, however, be misleading to present *apartheid* in terms solely of human rights.[2] It is fundamentally a network of legal provisions which, combined with the prohibition of African trade unions, has the effect of obliging the African to sell his labour at an unjust price. This alone accounts for the very high dividends which are possible. Either raw materials or capital equipment or management or labour must be in a unique position. The answer is that it is cheap labour that provides the differential. The *apartheid* system results in seven million economic helots. On this exploited labour the profitability of investment in South Africa depends; from this exploited labour are derived in part the £60,000,000 of dividends paid to British shareholders.[3]

44. This is strong language. But consider the facts set out in the following table:

Category	White South Africans	Black South Africans
Population (millions)	3·5	11·5
Per capita income (1959)	$1,819	$109
Average wage in mining (1962)*	$3,587	$216

* *Wages in South African Mining* 1962

Colour	Persons employed (thousands)	Total Wages (millions of dollars)	Wages per Worker (dollars)
White	63	226	3,587
Non-white	540	117	216

(Source: *Commerce and Industry*, Pretoria, South Africa, June 1963, pp. 612, 614.)

[1] See Appendix IX for details concerning Clause 17 of the General Law Amendment Act. This—the infamous 90-day clause—was re-promulgated for one year as from 30th June 1964, in spite of the protests of all the Churches represented in the Christian Council of South Africa, representatives of the Jewish and Islamic faiths, and many of the judiciary. (Suspended Jan. 1965.)

[2] For summary of *apartheid* legislation since 1950, see Appendix X, p. 123.

[3] An analogy with nineteenth-century profits from the slave trade is not misplaced. It will be remembered that the Great Trek took place in part because the British Government abolished slavery in the Cape and Natal in 1834.

Category	White South Africans	Black South Africans
Ages subject to tax	21–60	18–65
Income exempt from tax	$840	None
Education expenditure per pupil (1962)	$182	$18
Infant mortality per 1,000 births	27	200+
Percentage of population (Balance: Asian and mixed)	19	68
Percentage of land reserved	87	13
Persons in registered trade unions	340,000	None
Persons convicted of pass offences (1962)	None	384,000

(Sources: *State of South Africa: Economic, Financial and Statistical Yearbook for the Republic of South Africa*, Johannesburg, 1962 also *Report of the Special Committee on the Policies of Apartheid of the Government of the Republic of South Africa*, United Nations. General Assembly, 16th September, 1963.)

As the comparison between the white and African mining wage ($3,587 compared to $216 p.a.) is misleading, in so far as the managerial responsibility is white, the following comparison should be considered:

Average African mining wage in South Africa: $216 plus rations.

Average African mining wage in Northern Rhodesia: £810.

45. South Africa presents investment the attractive prospect of a modern, developed industrial society with three and a half million prosperous white customers, and a cheap labour supply of eleven and a half million black Africans who are prohibited by law from organizing unions, bargaining collectively, striking or moving without permission (they sometimes live as virtual prisoners in police compounds—rows of cramped cabins surrounded by high walls and barbed wire). No wonder Britain has £1,000,000,000 invested, no wonder American investment has increased in 1962 by $44,000,000—as much as the entire U.S. investment in 1945.[1] The whole issue of economic motivation in the policies of the British and American Governments must be borne in mind at all times concerning South Africa: which to say is not to deny the legitimacy of such motivation, but to realize the role it plays.

46. An important aspect of *apartheid* is to see it, not from our own white eyes, but from the point of view of the African father of a family, needing work to feed his children. Oliver Tambo, the Deputy Leader of the African National Congress, who was one of those who gave evidence to the Working Party, has put this forcibly in a way that most white South Africans never hear, let alone enter into:

'Abantwana balala ngendlala!' This is the anguished but all too familiar cry of a starving mother in South Africa's reserves, writing

---

[1] American profits have increased in proportion:

1959: $43,000,000		1961: $61,000,000	
1960: $50,000,000		1962: $72,000,000.	

to her husband, telling him that the children are starving. He is
working on a white farm, in competition with convict labour, or he
is in a mine receiving wages far below those enjoyed by white
miners, or maybe he is sweeping the streets of some city, and earn-
ing £3 a week, from which he pays for his food, rent, train or bus
fare to and from work, wherever he may be working. If he sends any
money, it is all spent within a few days of its receipt. His wife writes
a second letter reporting how many of the children are ill, and a
third one telling which of them has already died. But, precisely because the children are starving and dying of starvation, he must
remain working. He must find work and accept any wage.[1]

The reserves are overcrowded, poor, unproductive and are the
scene of perennial famines. He must seek work outside the reserves.
If he goes to the mines, he may never return, and if he does he may
bring back a broken limb or a miner's phthisis. If he goes to work on
a farm, there will be a sjambok and a boot urging him to work
harder and yet harder, and at the end of the contract his earnings
will have accumulated to a mere pittance. Where he offers himself
for either the mines or for farm labour, he will have little difficulty
in proceeding to his place of employment. His travelling expenses
will be met by way of a loan, to be recovered by compulsory deduc-
tion from his wages. But if, because of the unpopularity of the work
in the mines or on farms, he enters an urban area for the purpose of
seeking work, then from the time of such entry he is like a convict
at large, liable to be taken to the nearest prison on meeting the
first policeman; for the Urban Areas Act and the Pass Laws make
it practically impossible for him to escape arrest, unless he plays a
cat-and-mouse game with the police—spending the night in a wide
variety of backyards, taking illegal shelter with friends, if any, while
during the day, as he moves from place to place exploring various
avenues to lawful residence and employment, he avoids the police as
if they were carnivores waylaying their black-skinned booty at
street corners. The obstacles placed in the way of taking up a job
completely deprive the African of the power to bargain for satisfactory terms of employment and place him at the unrestricted
mercy of the employer.

47. It is true that the wages of the black labour force as a whole are
higher than elsewhere in Africa, which explains why some 800,000 are

[1] According to a statement made by the Chairman of the Bantu Wages and
Productivity Association on 30th October 1963, the average monthly income of
heads of households was R42.05 p.m. (£21·025). In 45·8 per cent of households,
the head is the sole breadwinner. As the poverty datum line has been calculated
at R46 p.m., there must be many families below it.

at present employed in South Africa, who came from the High Commission Territories, Mozambique, and further afield. But the equitable comparison is that between the differential of skills and the differential of wages within South Africa between white and black workers. The following figures are suggestive; they relate to the manufacturing industry as a whole.

Year	Average African Wage (p.a.)	Average White Wage (p.a.)	Ratio between the two wages
1946	£159	£734	1 : 4·6
1958	£173	£916	1 : 5·3
1961	£177	£991	1 : 5·6

Thus between 1946 and 1961 white earnings in the manufacturing industries rose by 35 per cent, African wages by 11 per cent. The rise in the cost of living in the same period far outstripped the rise in African wages. The comparative figures for the mining industry have already been given. In comparative terms the African mine worker receives one-sixteenth of the white worker's wages. The figure of $216 p.a. represents 3s. per shift, plus a ration of mealie meal, potatoes, some inexpensive meat and a few items produced on white farms, where African wages are even lower: one-seventeenth of the white earnings.

48. The overriding reason for this grim position is the stern necessity felt by the white population to maintain its political and economic domination of the country, and so safeguard its cultural identity. If the philosophy underlying separate development has more often been stated by Afrikaners, the practice of the colour bar lies as much at the door of the English-speaking members of the nation. Most English-speaking South Africans are now as much against black participation in civic rights as the Afrikaners. Such difference as there was at the time of the Union they have been slow to defend. In practice they accept Mr Strijdom's words when he removed the last of the non-white voters from the common voters' roll:

> Call it paramountcy, *baaskap*, or what you will, it is still domination. I am being as blunt as I can. I am making no excuses. Either the white man dominates or the black man takes over. . . . The only way the Europeans can maintain supremacy is by domination. . . . And the only way they can maintain domination is by withholding the vote from the non-Europeans.

49. In spite of growing doubts among a minority, many of the Afrikaner section of the population still hold the conviction that what is being done is right before God and is in the best interests of Africans

as well as Europeans. The majority believe it to be expedient. As Mr Strijdom also said:

> In our actions towards the non-whites in the application of our traditional policy of separation we shall have to act in such a way as to give proof that we are not hostile towards the non-whites; that separation is in the interests of both colour groups; and that with this policy clashes and friction are eliminated and co-existence but not integration is assured.

It is by this co-existence, this parallel development, that Afrikaners see the only way of safeguarding their own folkways after the long struggle which has turned them through the centuries from a settler-group to a nation, a nation unique in history for the speed with which its own national language has developed.[1] As they look back over their history they see Christian civilization given as a trust to their people from God, a trust of which he had given them proofs, as for example, in his help in victory over the Zulus on the Day of the Covenant. As they seek to safeguard their own nationalism they recognize the nationalism of African groups and see in the 'Bantustans' the only way, consistent with the maintaining of their own identity, of allowing national development and, ultimately, 'equal opportunity' to Africans. In so doing they seem to be projecting on to the different Bantu groups, Xhosas, Zulus and others, their own desire to live only within the world of their own language and their own traditions.

50. To men of such iron will and determination this '*apartheid*' is the only possible framework for the ordering of the nation. That is why all attempts by non-whites to obtain a share in the consultative processes of the state have been met with a blank refusal. The moderation and patience shown by the petitioners have been more than remarkable. When Chief Luthuli was given the choice by the Government in 1952 to resign from the African National Congress or forfeit his position as chief, in choosing to forego the latter, he said:

> Who will deny that thirty years of my life have been spent knocking in vain, patiently, moderately and modestly at a closed and barred door? What have been the fruits of moderation? The last thirty years have seen the greatest number of laws restricting our rights and progress, until today we have reached a stage where we almost have no right at all. It is with this background and with a full sense of responsibility that, under the auspices of the African National Congress, I have joined my people in the new spirit that

---

[1] 'By cutting us off from the Netherlands, you English made us a white tribe in Africa: we shall act like one', was an illuminating remark made recently by the editor of *Die Burger*.

moves them today, the spirit that revolts openly and boldly against injustice and expresses itself in a determined and non-violent manner.

51. Now the African Congresses have been banned and their leaders, including Chief Luthuli, silenced. Legitimate means of expression have been suppressed by harsh legislation, cruel penalties and police intimidation. Africans say that if their policy of non-violence is being replaced by violence, it is only in reply to the violence that has been done to them. There is no proper machinery for examining industrial grievances, and no right to non-whites to strike in support of their industrial claims. *The total effect is one of inexorable compression gradually creating conditions for a general explosion.* The truth of this general proposition is not invalidated because there are many individual cases of excellent personal relations between white and non-white South Africans.

52. We cannot close this short account of South Africa today without recording our respect for those of all races who are taking a stand on principles they know to be right and who have suffered, and are suffering, for their action, either at the hands of the state or of those of their own community.[1] It is upon such that depends the hope of reconciliation.

VI. CONDEMNATION OF APARTHEID IS NOT ENOUGH: WHAT ARE THE ALTERNATIVES?

53. We have sought to understand the fears of those in South Africa who are seeking to preserve their heritage. For some it is a political and cultural ethos. For others it is a privileged material position. For both it is a way of life which they believe menaced. We have to ask ourselves, however, whether a system can be justified if it carries with it so much mental and physical misery for such a large part of the population, and denies to adult men and women the freedom to share in decisions about their own life. Our answer can only be that we, with the Churches in South Africa, find it repugnant to the Christian belief in the dignity of God's children.

54. We are not alone in this judgment. In its *Statement on Racial and Ethnic Tension* of August 1963, the Central Committee of the World Council of Churches calls for a change. (See Appendix XI.) The political authorities have been equally forthright. The United Kingdom representative at the United Nations Security Council said on 6th August 1963:

> The racial policies of the Government of South Africa are entirely repugnant to my Government and to the feelings and traditions of our people.

[1] See also below, para. 135.

55. On three grounds, each of them sufficient in itself, we cannot be passive spectators in the present situation. The first is that increasing injustice is being experienced by our fellow men and women. The second is that our country is obliged to adopt a policy in the United Nations. The third is that the tension now building up in South Africa forms a potential threat to world peace. There is also the present responsibility of the United Kingdom arising out of the Act of Union in 1910.

56. It is not responsible, however, to call for the removal of the present restrictions on personal liberty and of those other requirements of *apartheid* to which objection is taken, without attempting to state constructively what policy is open to the South African Government in place of the position of white domination they are defending. What should such a policy be?

57. Those many Africans who have not yet despaired of finding a non-violent solution still ask for a round-table conference, a kind of national convention of representatives of all sections of the population, which will discuss how, and by what steps, the political power of the present State of South Africa can be more adequately shared. They realize that this is impossible without a change of mind in the Government. As an African leader said recently: 'The Government and its supporters are so sure that they know what is good for us; they also know what we want, they know equally well that we can't have it; therefore no useful purpose would be served by any discussion whatever.' We, too, realize that the Government will only be ready to attend such a conference when it has been brought to the point of recognizing that an alternative to *apartheid* must be found. This is, nevertheless, what we would envisage, that *the Government of South Africa should call a conference of leaders of all sections of the country*.

58. Although it is not for us to say what answer a round-table conference would give to the question facing it, we may rightly be asked what are, in our view, the possibilities open to it. We have already said that *apartheid*, or white domination, is not acceptable to the Christian conscience. *Neither would a black domination which sought in the opposite way to deny to whites equal civic and cultural rights.* There remain three other possible patterns, and only three:

(i) *Partition;*

(ii) *Federation, or confederation*, of a number of separate, homogeneous states;

(iii) *Integration*, i.e. a unitary state with equal rights for all, whether they are of a majority or minority group.

59. In examining these three patterns, we believe that whichever is finally adopted must include the following elements if it is to be morally acceptable:

the recognition of human rights and respect of human dignity for individuals of all races within any South African state or states, whether members of a majority or a minority, and whether nationals or not of the state concerned;

the right of all communities to preserve and develop their own ethos and institutions, within the general interest of the whole;

the provision of a tolerable livelihood together with rapid educational, political and economic advancement for the less developed sections of the community, whether these are part of a unitary, federal or independent state.

Partition

60. It is possible to envisage the creation of two separate and independent states, one largely white, the other largely non-white, with some attempt at equity in the division of resources between them. It is doubtful whether a division of land on a purely historical basis is either possible or just. The present reserves are, in the words of Leo Marquardi 'for the most part of the shrunken remnant of the land once owned by the tribes'. Much of the 'white' land was not virgin, but was ceded to the whites after conquest or by treaties which in the African mind intended the grant of customary usage and not ownership. Professor Monica Wilson's historical study shows that in much of 'white' territory it was Africans who arrived and settled first.[1] Any division would also have to take into account some sharing of mineral and industrial resources; only a fair division would ensure future peaceful coexistence between the white and non-white states. This would result in a much more painful partition of the country for whites than under the existing Bantustan policy, for they would have to bear more of the anguish of upheaval which to date is being borne mainly by the non-whites. Further, any plan for partition would have to find an acceptable place for the Coloureds and Asians. In fulfilment of the first provision of the preceding paragraph, it would be necessary to grant to any non-white living in the white state a civic status comparable to that of Eire citizens in the United Kingdom, and vice versa.

61. Most economists and industrialists are against partition. They believe it would do irreparable harm to South Africa's industry and to what is economically a well-defined geographical entity. Any plan for partition would have to effect a compromise between two different criteria: the requirements of human society in terms of distributive justice, and the requirements of economic life.[2] As the latter reflect unalterable

[1] Cp. e.g. 'The Early History of Transkei and Ciskei', *African Studies*, vol. 18, No. 4.
[2] Cp. para. 26 above.

D

factors such as the location of raw materials, such a compromise would necessarily, to some extent, both inhibit justice and reduce wealth.

62. Articulate Africans are totally opposed to the idea. They reject the basic philosophy of the whites, opposing strenuously any suggestion that a part of South Africa should be earmarked for a particular racial group. They reject also the view that the 'white' parts of South Africa are not just as much their home as the reserves. They do not accept the white view as expressed by Hertzog;

> Nobody compels the Native to settle in this country, but if he does so it is demanded from him that he should respect the white man and obey the laws of the country.

Their claim is for a fair share in the United South Africa of which they are an integral part; as Dr Z. K. Matthews has said:

> We are not opposed to the white man or anyone else claiming for themselves in the land which they have made their home all the fundamental rights to which as human beings they are entitled. What we cannot concede is that this is a claim of which the white man has a monoply.

Africans from other parts of the continent are as rigidly opposed to partition, for they are resolved to wipe out the colour bar, and suspect any proposal for the formation of a new, if smaller, white South Africa as indicating a perpetuation of the present race discrimination.

63. The United Nations Expert Committee rejected partition on the following grounds as we have seen:[1]

> No line of partition could be established by agreement and an imposed partition would create a long frontier of continuing conflict. Nor could partition be politically or economically viable, for there is no substantial area of South Africa in which there is a majority of whites, and the economy of South Africa, both in industry and agriculture, is entirely dependent on non-white labour. Partition would not solve, but would intensify and aggravate, racial conflict.

64. Nevertheless, we have been reminded of the many cases of partition which have taken place in this century, both in Europe and Asia. Where there has been complete deadlock between two communities the only possible course has been to undertake a major surgical operation, carried out to the hurt of many people, but representing a smaller price to pay than continued friction and bloodshed. If the white people of South Africa insist on maintaining some form of white domination, or the Afrikaner group among them seek an exclusive home for

---

[1] Para. 34 of the Introduction.

their culture, then partition and large-scale transfers of population may have to be the last resort. It cannot be welcomed. Nevertheless, conditions might become such in South Africa as to make it the only recourse. History would show whether the new Africa would indefinitely accept— or the inhabitants be able to sustain—such a white enclave at the continent's southern tip.

Federation or Confederation

65. One suggestion put forward within South Africa which would allow for partial separation is for the creation of some dozen or more states in a federation or confederation. By an appropriate drawing of boundaries, most of the states would comprise a large majority of one racial group, though some, including the Rand, would have to be designated 'non-racial'. This plan would provide opportunity for the main characteristics of the majority of any state to find expression within its internal government, educational system and social development. In a federal system there would have to be weighted representation in the Federal Parliament to meet the fears of the minorities, and provision for the guarantee of human and ethnic rights in the Federal Constitution.

66. The United Nations Expert Committee favours a federal solution, chiefly because it would provide a guarantee against the overriding of democratic rights by the central government; foster local co-operation, and make possible the membership of South-West Africa and the present High Commission Territories. But this is envisaged on a specifically non-racial basis.

> We wish to make it clear that in our view representation should not be on any racial basis, but on the basis of national or regional representation through a fully democratic franchise on a common voters' roll.[1]

As it is precisely the racial issue which is the cause of the cleavage, this variety of federal system with racial integration presents the same problem as the unitary state of a racially integrated character which is examined in the next section.

67. The Expert Committee seems to have concentrated on the wrong aspect of federalism in this context. It is neither the checks and balances of a federal constitution nor the relative rights of central and regional government that are the key here. It is the possibility federalism provides of differing peoples cohabiting and co-operating to a degree defined in advance in a written constitution. Of course, modern federations tend to be centripetal, because of the increasing role of the state (e.g. social services). But residuary powers can be reserved to constituent states. The great virtue of a federation is that it maintains a single cus-

[1] Para. 56 of the U.N. report.

toms area: thus both common economic interest and diversified racial composition are simultaneously reflected.

68. A federal system—though the fruit of centuries of constitutional wisdom and experience[1]—is no panacea, however, but simply a political device which will work provided the citizens desire to be united but not unitary. Therefore, precisely in so far as it maintains links which partition would sever, it presupposes a readiness on the part of the ethnic groups in South Africa to co-operate on a basis of equality, because of a recognized common interest. Unless the principle of such co-operation were accepted by both white and black, such a system could neither be established nor long survive if the attempt were made to set it up.

69. The same basic need for a will to live and work together to a recognized extent must be true of a confederation, though this is a looser system, where sovereignty resides eventually with the member states. In modern society, a confederation is really an anachronism, a stepping-stone to federation or to nothing. Otherwise it may be little more than a permanent association of states with a central 'government' entirely dependent on those of the member states. In this sense NATO in 1951-53, when Stalin made the Soviet threat imminent, was a confederation in the military sphere. The European Economic Community will, in the economic sphere, be more than a confederation when the transitional phases laid down in the Treaty of Rome have been completed, because of the supranational voting that will then obtain. The nice—and disputed—distinction between federation and confederation need not delay us: the relevant issue here is that both represent more unity than partition, less unity than a unitary state. They therefore have all the merits and defects of a compromise; their virtue is the realism of corresponding to a given phase of preparedness to co-operate. Where the differences between the citizens are deep, there is no reason why the phase should not be semi-permanent, providing always the will to be united (but not unitary) remains.

Integration in a Unitary State[2]

70. If this is the intention it must aim at a democratic society in which human freedom and political and economic rights are afforded to all men and women irrespective of race, colour or creed. This is what the non-white South Africans ask for, and the white South Africans fear. In their requests, the non-whites have been envisaging a genuine non-

[1] For a more detailed examination of the unitary, not federal, character of the Union of 1910, see Appendix XIV. In this context the constitution of the Union provides no precedent, only a warning.

[2] That is a unitary state with equal rights for all. Integration does not necessarily mean miscegenation, which most whites fear, but which black South Africans do not want. But clearly marriage between adults of different racial groups must be permissible in such a state.

racial country in which there could be equal rights for all; they have not been speaking of black domination. It has to be recognized, however, that the long history of the disregard of their requests has recently led to a harder tone among some of them and to the demand for immediate universal adult suffrage, which would, in effect, mean immediate black control. A way has to be found of so sharing power that the giving up of domination does not mean being dominated. For integration to succeed there must be security for both white and black to share in and contribute to a developing culture. Is there any way by which safeguards can be arranged to achieve this? However carefully safeguards are written into a constitution, they are never wholly effective if the Executive is determined to override or circumvent them. Mr Strijdom, by his packing both of the Senate and the Court of Appeal in order to eliminate the the Coloured vote in the Cape, has already shown how such safeguards can be overturned. Constitutional safeguards, therefore, with the establishment of a Bill of Human Rights, and a Supreme Court, as proposed by the U.N. Expert Committee, would seem to require underwriting by international guarantee.[1]

71. Professor Cowen, in his book *The Foundations of Freedom*, not only discusses the subject of safeguards, but also the preparation that ought now to be taking place for integration. He gives a salutary reminder that attitudes will not change overnight following the adoption of a constitution, and outlines something of the slow process by which the racial myths of today might be dispersed. While this is happening, a form of franchise will be necessary that gives opportunity for active non-white participation in government yet, at the same time, gives assurance to whites so that a non-racial democracy can grow steadily and happily.

[1] International law has made enormous strides in the area of human rights since the war. The European Convention on Human Rights and Fundamental Freedoms is the most advanced example. Attempts are being made at the moment to prepare a similar Convention for Africa. Such regional agreements can go much further than is yet possible on a world level, because there is greater readiness for the surrender of sovereignty which is necessarily involved. It is from Europe, too, that comes the most recent example of the international guarantee of human rights being a fundamental element in reaching agreement over an area in which there were two major elements in the population: a minority supported by one neighbouring country, a majority supported by another neighbouring country. This is the Saar. As proposed by the Council of Europe in the European Statute of the Saar of 1954, Article 19 laid down that the Settlement would be guaranteed, not only by the Governments of France, the German Federal Republic, but also by the United Kingdom and the United States of America. Part of the Constitution so guaranteed was Article 16, which abolished the 'licensing of political parties, associations, newspapers and public meetings'. This had the effect of adding a United States guarantee to the implementation in the Saar of the European Convention of Human Rights, of which the Saar had been a signatory, and of the further provision of Article 16 quoted above (i.e. no right of derogation in respect of political parties, as permitted under Article 15 of the Convention 'in time of public emergency').

72. At this point we believe that the initiative taken by the representative of Norway in the United Nations Security Council is of importance. The resolution adopted on his motion on 4th December 1963 refers to

> resolving the present situation in South Africa through full, peaceful and orderly application of human rights and fundamental freedoms to all inhabitants of the territory as a whole, regardless of race, colour or creed, and to consider what parts the United Nations might play in the achievement of that end.

73. There is still hope for a meeting of the communities in South Africa. We see two points of common ground which we believe could form a new growing point:

(i) Large numbers of South Africans, of all races, feel passionately that South Africa, within the boundaries history has given it, is their home and they are unwilling to see it carved up. This is a sentiment of love and, as such, the seed from which a just solution might grow.

(ii) Both whites and non-whites are passionately concerned to safeguard the happiness of their children. Is there not here a point of common humanity which, in calling from parents for sacrifice for their children, could guide that sacrifice into mutually respecting channels?

74. We would repeat that we are sure that whatever solution is found must be a South African solution. We have tried to indicate the courses which may be open. We would, however, put a question to those who are sensitive to the two points mentioned above:

> What sacrifice are you prepared to make to preserve the unity of the land of South Africa for your children?

The whites would have to concede equality of human, if not at first all civil, rights; the non-whites would have to be content with a progressive —if rapid—transition towards universal suffrage and a better standard of living. Such willingness may seem unlikely, but it is for such changes of heart that we must hope, work and pray. To discount them is to discount the measure of God's mercy and the power of His grace.

VII. THE URGENCY OF THE SITUATION

75. Within South Africa there is increasing tension. The Government of Dr Verwoerd has felt it necessary to increase heavily the numbers and cost of the police and of the armed forces.[1] Among non-whites

---

[1] In the decade 1948 to 1958, the average annual defence budget was below £20,000,000. *In the subsequent five years it has quadrupled, and now amounts to 12 per cent of the national revenue.* The Government announced in June 1964 that the Defence Budget for 1964–5 is to reach a record figure of £115,000,000, which is £30,000,000 more than during the preceding year. It includes special

there is increasing resentment, however little opportunity it may have for expression. Acts of sabotage are increasing. Despite the stern action taken against opposition groups and the difficulty of organization they face, those who have decided to turn to violent methods are likely to find ways for further acts of violence. To state this is not to condone violence. The Archbishop of Durban, the Most Rev. Denis E. Hurley, when asked by the *Rand Daily Mail* recently,

What is your view, or Christianity's view, of the increasing trend towards political violence among non-whites?

replied:

I can only deplore it. Although Christians in the past were responsible for a fair amount of violence, Christianity itself is opposed to violence. But if Christians fail to offer a positive solution to our racial problems, a solution inspired by deep religious principles, they will have little reason to complain if violence is turned against them.

At the risk of it being thought that Christians in the United Kingdom are supporting violence in South Africa, it seems to us that an additional point has also to be made. Unless we accept the full pacifist position ourselves and reserve no right to use force to defend ourselves

---

supplementary estimates for the purchase of heavy arms such as warships, aircraft, tanks and armoured cars. Among the aircraft for which this money is required is the order for Buccaneer Mk II naval strike 'planes, which are to be supplied by Great Britain unless there is a change as a result of the General Election.

The Government White Paper states that there is a wide programme for extending existing military airfields and building new strategic airfields in various parts of South Africa. In addition, defence materials and fuels are to be stockpiled at strategic centres.

In the Budget for 1964–5 is included the figure of £16,500,000 for the manufacture of munitions in South Africa.This figure is one hundred times more than the figure in 1960, when it was only £107,000. The reason given in the White Paper for this was the difficulty in buying munitions overseas. A military aircraft factory has just been completed.

The global figures for defence expenditure of R230 million in 1964–65 may be compared with the following figures for the last four preceding years:

1960–61	R35 million
1961–62	R72 million
1962–63	R125 million
1963–64	R171·5 million

Land forces available as a result of this expenditure are given in the Defence White Paper, published on 6th June 1964, as follows:

Regulars: 14,926 officers and men.

Citizen force: 70,000 (9 months' compulsory service, and subsequently on 72 hours' call). Intake 16,527 per year.

Commandos: 51,487 (weekend units, but equipped with automatic weapons).

Police: 12,000 whites (+10,000 reserves) and 13,700 non-whites.

See also Appendix XII, p. 127.

against possible totalitarian domination, we have no moral right to deny to non-whites within the Republic of South Africa the right to resistance by force. In a world in which national sovereignty is gradually giving way, and must more quickly give way, to the world rule of law, it is becoming increasingly difficult to invoke the sanctity of national sovereignty if the sanctity of the individual as set out in the Universal Declaration of Human Rights is persistently violated.

76. This is no academic question. At the moment, sabotage is taking place in South Africa. It has not been deterred by the sentences of life imprisonment passed on Nelson Mandela and his associates, who stated in their defence that they had been driven to selected acts of sabotage as the only form of political expression left to them. Elsewhere in the continent, the states of North, East and West Africa have declared their intention of wiping out *apartheid* by force. The Emperor Haile Selassie, speaking at the Summit Conference of African Heads of State in Addis Ababa in May 1963, said,

> We rededicate ourselves to the elimination of racial discrimination from this continent . . . racial discrimination is a denial of the personality and dignity which we have struggled to establish for ourselves as Africans.

Within a year, the increased repression in South Africa, and the reluctance of Britain and the U.S.A. to bring pressure to bear, led the Kenyan Minister of Home Affairs, Mr Oginga Odinga, to state in Peking in May 1964:

> The remaining colonial territories in Africa will not be liberated until the independent African states jointly are prepared to wage war, I repeat war, against South Africa.[1]

77. The Organization of African Unity established a Fund for the Assistance of Liberation Movements, with the purpose of armed intervention. To this the Addis Ababa powers are contributing 1 per cent of their revenue.[2] In Algeria, 10,000 troops are being trained for operations against South Africa. At Dar-es-Salaam, a further force of 3,000 'freedom fighters' is undergoing intensive training, under Dr Mond-

---

[1] This was no isolated outburst to please Mr Odinga's hosts. In Nairobi on 21st June, four Kenya Ministers, led by the Minister of Justice, 'buried' a symbolic coffin containing the 'remains' of the Prime Minister of South Africa and of *apartheid*. Mr Kenyatta then said to the applauding crowd,

Kenya has won her freedom, but this is nothing if our brothers still suffer under the colonial yoke in South Africa. Even if it means bloodshed, we must get rid of the *apartheid* Government of South Africa. . . . I only pray that Verwoerd and his fellow-racists will not goad and goad the Africans to the point where the nationalist movement is driven to oppose the white man as such.

[2] At the Cairo Conference in July 1964 it was stated that some African states were defaulting on these payments.

lane. (However, the first objective of the Tanganyikan 'Army of Liberation' is to launch a major guerrilla warfare operation in the wild and
mountainous area of the Maconde in N. Mozambique; this may soon
begin.) The African states concerned may be unrealistic regarding the
outcome of a pitting of their small and unco-ordinated armed forces
over vast distances through a difficult terrain with no adequate line of
communications against the considerable land and air forces of South
Africa.[1] The latter have the best of modern weapons, purchased
chiefly from Great Britain and France. They are supplied as to ammunition from South Africa's growing arms industry. They have the advantage of defending interior lines well supported by rail and road communications. The African states, however, are resolved that the affront to
black dignity shall cease. It is for them the symbol of all they have
suffered at the hands of the white man in the past.[2] It would be unrealistic to underestimate the strength of this resolve. There comes to mind
a quiet, elderly church leader from Nigeria speaking moderately but
passionately of the indignities he and others suffered at Jan Smuts Air-
port when travelling from Lagos to Salisbury. Such people can enter
into the experience of the millions of their own race in South Africa in a
way that Europeans cannot. There has been aroused in the rest of Africa
a moral indignation for which as a world force there is no exact parallel.
The crusade now being launched will not be held back by present
material odds. What therefore has to be faced is that there will be attempts at military action against South Africa; that, however unlikely
they may be at first to succeed, they will lead inevitably to increasing
para-military involvement of the Eastern and Western blocs, with the
real possibility of the world conflict to which a magnified Congo-type
situation could lead.

78. Therefore, while it is true that military judgment in 1964-65
is that the rest of Africa could not alone coerce its southern tip if the
ring is kept clear, political judgment cannot say so readily that a race
war, once started, could be confined to the African continent. This is
the reason for the sense of urgency felt at the United Nations, and why
we find ourselves compelled to ask whether there is any pressure short
of war by which the deadlock between the communities in South Africa
can be broken. It was for this reason the British Council of Churches,
in October 1963, made the issue of sanctions a principal part of the
remit to the International Department.

79. Before we attempt to fulfil this instruction, with all the reluctance of Christians obliged to enter a realm where they feel ill at ease, a

---

[1] See also Appendix XII, p. 127.
[2] '*Apartheid* is the most abominable symbol of the worst humiliations which
for centuries have been imposed upon Africa' (The Secretary-General of the
Organization of African Unity).

word must be said about the effects of the present economic boom in South Africa.[1]

80. The facts are startling. Measured from South Africa's currency crisis of mid-1961, when the flight of non-resident funds was checked at the eleventh hour by capital controls, by September 1964 the upswing in business had lasted a record 39 months, and shows every sign of continuing into 1965. In 1963, helped by the additional spending of 30,000 immigrants, retail sales recorded a 9 per cent increase on 1962. Imports rose by 24 per cent. Industrialists must have been prepared to spend heavily on extensions to plant and equipment to make this possible. Private fixed investment outlay rose by $12\frac{1}{2}$ per cent in 1963 over the previous year, and fixed investment by government and semi-government undertakings by 17 per cent. There was an 8 per cent increase in real national product (9 per cent in money terms), following the rise of $5\frac{1}{2}$ per cent in 1962. Company profits for 1962-63 were 30 per cent up on 1961-62. At the end of 1963, foreign reserves were $763,000,000, compared with only $216,000,000 in mid-1961, and showing an increase of $118,000,000 in 1963 alone, despite the substantial increase in imports. 'This was a remarkable performance for the South African economy. Traditionally an upturn in business has been accompanied by a downturn in the foreign reserves. . . . This is a dramatically different picture from the one drawn of South Africa less than three years ago.'[2]

81. South Africa's economic boom looks as if it has entered the second, investment, stage on a strong footing. Ample credit is available in the banking system to finance a high level of production, and there is ample risk capital to supplement the higher plough-backs from current earnings. An impressive number of major projects is planned, including two new gold mines, development of a new source of platinum, a new steel plant, new industries for producing synthetic rubber, plastics and fertilizers, and a big ship-building yard. A number of motor companies are intending to set up factories for the complete manufacture in South Africa of their cars, which in the past have only been assembled in the Union. The still buoyant level of gold output and the firm trend in most of South Africa's export commodites should enable export earnings to keep pace easily with the further rise in imports expected in 1965. Direct private investment by foreigners has increased substantially, to the great encouragement of Dr Verwoerd's Government.

82. 'Today businessmen have almost forgotten the shock of Sharpeville in 1960 and South Africa's exit from the Commonwealth; they readily shrug off the vulnerability of South-West Africa; and optimistically disregard the deterioration in the Republic's external relations. They even find justification for Dr Verwoerd's "granite" policies in

[1] Cp. also paras 89–91 below.
[2] *The Economist*, 7th March, 1964.

reports of deep-seated instability and diminishing freedom and democracy in the rest of the African continent.'[1] The country's prosperity even led the Roman Catholic Archbishop of Bloemfontein to state in March 1964:

> It is clear that the South African situation, despite its defects, is stable, secure and full of prospects for future development.

Some believe that this extraordinary boom may seriously erode the Government's restrictive labour policies, in practice if not in principle. By job fragmentation and work reorganization new operations will be designed to which the colour bar does not apply, and against which neither the white trade unions nor the Minister of Labour are likely to protest. 'In this way the exponents of *apartheid* can avoid loss of face, industry will avoid loss of productivity, and the economy may, in practice, largely escape being slowed down to the rate of growth of the white labour force supplemented by immigration.' Those who place their faith in the consequences of the economic boom hope that the shared prosperity which South Africa's economy is capable of generating 'may yet succeed in vanquishing *apartheid*, where political pressure, passive resistance and sabotage have so far failed'.[2]

83. As against this, the Working Group considered that the argument of the economic solvent of race discrimination was misleading, and largely illusory, in that it has been advanced for the last forty years, during which time the rights of the African had been steadily reduced, not increased. The point is further considered in paragraphs 89 and 91 below.

84. This boom does not mean, however, that the Africans are sharing fairly in this new wealth, nor that, in so far as their material standards may rise, they represent less potentially inflammatory human material. The French Revolution began when the graph of human misery and despair was turning upwards. In 1789, there were no outside states ready to aid the revolutionaries; on the contrary, the Allies invaded France to restore the monarchy. In the mid-1960s, it is the external forces that hold the key. To their potential capacity and resolve for action we must now turn.

VIII. ECONOMIC SANCTIONS

85. The conclusions we have reached in the previous two sections are:

(i) that the policy of the present Government of South Africa towards its African, Coloured and Asian citizens is morally and politically unacceptable;

[1] *The Economist, ibid.*   [2] *The Economist, ibid.*

(ii) that whatever may be the ultimate solution of the problem of inter-racial relationships in that country, the solution should be worked out within South Africa by representatives of all the communities;

(iii) that a first step to this end is the calling of a round-table conference, which should be the immediate aim of any action for which friends of South Africa seek to press.

A. *The Arguments for Economic Sanctions*

86. It is clear that the calling of a conference is inconsistent with the basic tenets of South Africa's present policy. It seems impossible to avoid the conclusion that the South African Government as at present constituted will not change its policies voluntarily and that there is no immediate likelihood of its losing its support at the polls, on the basis of the present franchise.

87. How then can the aim be achieved? The United Kingdom representative has used these words in the Security Council:

> We believe that governments should continue to exert the maximum pressure possible and to use whatever methods they think appropriate and which are consistent with the Charter, to persuade the Government of South Africa to change its racial policies before it is too late.[1]

What methods are available, and what is their effect likely to be?

Diplomatic Pressure

88. The diplomatic pressure, which has been consistently brought to bear by our own Government in recent years, and which was reflected in Mr Macmillan's speech in Cape Town in 1960, has effected no substantial change. On the contrary, Dr Verwoerd preferred to leave the Commonwealth, and further and more drastic measures have been taken each year to implement the present policy. There is no hope from future bilateral diplomatic intervention on the major issue: all that could be done has been tried.

Economic Prosperity

89. There are those who believe that the surest way of effecting liberal penetration is through the strengthening of South Africa's economy. There are two lines of reasoning here. In responding to economic trends, industrialists find it necessary to pay better wages to non-whites and to help more of them to become skilled craftsmen. They also demand the most economic location of industry. They are therefore becoming dissatisfied with much of the outworking of the present separate development policy and will, it is argued, become more so in

[1] August, 1963.

future. A further boost to South African economy would accelerate this process and bring nearer the time when their influence decisively affects government policy.

90. The second point is more general. The greater exchange of goods and services between nations is an essential part of building a united world. It is the declared policy of the United Nations, and its importance was underlined at this year's United Nations' Conference on Trade and Development at Geneva.[1] Anything which interferes with this process, and with the associated exchange of ideas, in relation to South Africa, will only tend to the further isolation of white South African thinking. Similarly, in this view, cultural and sporting sanctions, though protesting in a way more likely to touch South Africa's feelings than perhaps any other, lose a valuable opportunity of the meeting of minds.

91. The difficulty about the point of view expressed in paragraph 89, which has been put forward for many years, is that it has not been borne out by experience. As has been pointed out (para. 83), similar economic forces have been operating since 1910, but without bringing about any such changes. We have therefore reluctantly come to the view that there is no time to await such developments. Moreover, there are yet few signs that the present economy has moved the industrial leaders to exercise any successful influence on their Government.

Economic Hardship

92. We therefore find ourselves forced to ask whether there are other forms of pressure short of war, though with grave consequences both within and outside South Africa, which might induce the present South African Government, or a successor government, to be willing at last to talk with African, Coloured and Asian leaders. It has been proposed in the United Nations that such pressure could take the form of economic sanctions which, it is argued, is the last course open short of war.[2]

[1] Thus the report of the Fifth Committee (Expansion of international trade and regional economic groupings), which was approved by the Conference in June 1964, lays down the following five principles, of which the second is particularly relevant:
  1. Economic relations between countries shall be based on respect for the principle of sovereign equality of States;
  2. *There shall be no discrimination on the basis of differences in socio-economic systems;*
  3. Every country has the sovereign right to trade freely and to dispose freely of its natural resources;
  4. Economic and social progress should be the concern of the international community and should help strengthen peaceful relations and co-operation among nations;
  5. National and international economic policies should be directed towards the attainment of an international division of labour.
[2] Cp. statement by the Chairman of the U.N. Special Committee on the Policies of *Apartheid* of the Government of South Africa, in April 1964:
  There are, and can be, only two kinds of solution: a peaceful one, for which Africans earnestly hope, or one based on violence, war and the useless

93. Instinctively we are against economic sanctions. We shrink from forcing our judgments on others, however much we may think the other person's view to be wrong. Economic sanctions are a form of police action. Are there any conditions under which such police action would be justified, as being a lesser evil than war? We suggest the following:

    (i) When it is necessary to uphold the rule of law;

    (ii) When all attempts at persuasion through discussion have failed;

    (iii) When the alternative seems to be the risk of armed conflict which might not prove capable of being contained;

    (iv) When the objective is clearly stated;

    (v) When a necessary condition for a 'just war' in Catholic theology can be met, namely that there is *reasonable likelihood of the required objective being attained.*

94. What are the arguments in favour of economic sanctions in the case of South Africa? Since white domination is not just an element in, but is the basis of, policy, the only hope of change is through events which make a majority of the white voters lose confidence in the Government's ability to carry out its policy. Many believe economic sanctions which interrupt the life of the country are the only method short of war capable of achieving this end. White people within South Africa have said that the only way they can see of the system of white supremacy collapsing is if strong pressure is brought to bear on the Government from outside the country as well as from within. They think it necessary that the will of the present Government should crack, and this can only happen, humanly speaking, through quite extreme pressure from outside. The purpose of such pressure would be to bring home to those sections of the white population which provide the backbone of support for the Nationalist Government that *apartheid* was leading not to their prosperity but to their ruin. After an initial stage of solidarity with the Government, this would lead the business world into opposition and the Afrikaans-speaking farmers into hesitancy, from which new political alignments could emerge.[1]

---

shedding of blood in a foredoomed cause . . . the choice is between economic sanctions and war.

A similar view was expressed by the U.N. Expert Committee, in relation to its own proposal for economic sanctions in the event of the South African Government refusing to convene the national convention the report proposes (cp. paras 131–132 of that report).

[1] Cp. words from an address given to the South African Institute of Race Relations, January 1964, by Leo Katzen, 'Implications of Economic and other Boycotts for South Africa':

A growth in the *laager* mentality seems to be the most likely reponse to pressures from outside, at least in the short run. But the combined effect of various boycotts is bound to make life increasingly less comfortable in South Africa. Is there likely to be a point, short of armed intervention from outside

95. Arguments against sanctions include the following:

(i) Like all previous outside criticism of the Government, they will only serve to drive the white peoples closer together;

(ii) That they will cause most harm to the people we are trying to help, the non-whites—though leaders of the latter have said they are ready to face the consequences;[1]

(iii) In the present state of international law, the legal arguments for sanctions against South Africa are tenuous (cp. paras. 117-123 below);

(iv) They could not be effectively carried out, or if they were, achieve their aim.

96. Those who advocate sanctions emphasize that *the situation is such that there is no easy solution. The problem is to choose between different courses of action which are all difficult, and will all have harsh consequences.* What was generally agreed in the Working Party was that the consequent temptation to inaction must be resisted, because the situation is growing worse. This is particularly true for the British Government, which has a greater temptation to immobility than any other, precisely because it does involve such a conflict of legitimate national interests.

97. We have in fact to recognize that Britain is in the unenviable position of being at the focal point of decision. Precisely because this country has the deepest historic ties, and the greatest trade with and investment in South Africa, no action can be taken by the United Nations without Britain's active support. The U.S.A. will not move without the U.K., and without the Anglo-Saxon powers not only the Security Council cannot take a unanimous decision, but no decision could be implemented. In political terms, we are inexorably being pressed towards an open choice between the African (and Asian) members of the Commonwealth and United Nations, and the white population of South Africa, many of whom are of British stock, in so far as they maintain *apartheid.* In moral terms, we are faced with a choice which for many Christians is yet more difficult.

98. We have emphasized in para. 77 that we do not think the determination behind what African states regard as a crusade should be underestimated; nor do we think it relevant that some of those states are themselves open to serious criticism. We believe that wisdom for our

or internal insurrection, at which those who support the political ideology (which is the cause of the growing isolation) feel they will be worse off than if that ideology were discarded?

[1] 'I am not greatly impressed when some who show this sudden concern for the non-white people in South Africa are the very people who have grown wealthy on poorly-paid labour. Then I am not merely puzzled. I am shocked by their hypocrisy' (the Rt Rev. Ambrose Reeves, formerly Bishop of Johannesburg, before the U.N. Special Committee on *Apartheid*).

Government lies in showing that it is prepared to act as well as to speak regarding South Africa's internal policy; in that way her influence could be used to ensure that acts of other countries were strictly limited and directed to the most helpful ends.

99. What form should this action take? Diplomatic exchange and public expression of opinion have been tried over a long period; they have shown that only pressure which goes beyond this is now likely to lead to results. The deteriorating situation—in particular internationally —requires action. A form of action which has been widely advocated (and nothing else has been) is economic sanctions.

100. This was brought to a head by the debate in the Security Council in June 1964, arising from the consideration of the report by the U.N. Expert Committee, already referred to. At its close, on the 18th June, Britain joined the United States, Bolivia, China, the Ivory Coast, Morocco, Norway and Brazil in voting for a resolution sponsored by the two latter powers, under which an Expert Committee has now been set up comprised of representatives of all eleven members of the Council (at the vote, France, Czechoslovakia and the Soviet Union had abstained for opposing reasons). The mandate of this Committee is to:

> undertake a technical and practical study and report to the Security Council as to the feasibility, effectiveness and implications of measures which could, as appropriate, be taken by the Security Council under the United Nations' Charter.

All members of the U.N. have been requested to co-operate with and submit their views to the Expert Committee by 30th November. The Committee must then submit its report to the Security Council not later than the 28th February, 1965.

101. It is true the U.K. Permanent Representative, Sir Patrick Dean, when voting for the resolution, added:

> In voting for the Resolution and participating in the study to be undertaken by the Expert Committee, Her Majesty's Government are in no sense committed now or at any time in the future to support measures of coercion against South Africa.

But the fact remains, not only that by voting for the study to be made at all, and not abstaining or using the veto, the U.K. has moved one step nearer the 'moment of truth', but that at the most a few months will elapse before the representative of an Administration freshly returned from the polls may have, in the name of the British people, to vote for, abstain, or veto a resolution in favour of sanctions based on detailed proposals. It is worthy of note that the timing of the recomposed[1] Security Council's discussion of the Expert Committee's report may con-

---

[1] The Netherlands may become a member.

ceivably run close to the judgment handed down by the International Court of Justice concerning South-West Africa.

102. For the reasons given in para. 97, Britain's responsibility will be the crucial one.[1] It was the initial view of the majority of the Working Party that a decision in favour of sanctions by the United Kingdom might merit support *if* it could be carried out in the following context:

(i) That it is United Nations policy observed by all member states;

(ii) That the limited aim should be the bringing about of discussions[2] in South Africa on a specific agenda;

(iii) That the measures proposed should be such as seem likely to bring the most effective pressure quickly to bear, so that they can be as quickly ended when the aim has been achieved.

Subsequently, however, the Working Party had the opportunity of confronting theory with the economic and logistic facts of the situation, as the Security Council will do when it receives the report of its Expert Committee. The source material for the study was derived from a detailed analysis of the findings of the 'International Conference on economic sanctions against South Africa' which met in London in April 1964 to examine a series of papers in all the relevant fields, prepared by experts during the preceding months. Our conclusions are set out in the following section.

B. *The Practicability of Economic Sanctions*

103. It has been suggested in the preceding section that any coercive measures must be likely to achieve the envisaged objective, and must bring effective pressure to bear quickly, so that they can be as quickly ended when the aim has been achieved.[3]

104. The first need is to establish the degree of resolve of the present Government of South Africa and their supporters to resist the declared purpose of sanctions, namely a round-table conference (cp. para. 57 above). Here there are two differing views.

105. The first is the absolutist, pessimist view; it has strong evidence to support it. Before Afrikaner leaders could take part in such a conference—or their participation be meaningful—they would in fact have to be prepared to abandon the principle of white domination and economic exploitation, and replace it by that of progressively established partnership (cp. para. 73 above). To them this would represent a re-

---

[1] For details of Britain's dominant trading position with South Africa, see Appendix XVI, p. 140.

[2] Cp. para. 57 above.

[3] Cp. Report of the U.N. Expert Committee to the Secretary-General, (para. 109): 'The tests to be applied in deciding these questions are the tests of speedy decision, full co-operation and effective implementation, the overriding purpose being to achieve a rapid transformation with a minimum of suffering and dislocation.'

E

versal of their history, an abandonment of their most cherished belief, a revolution in their whole present way of life, and the end of Afrikaner nationalism, with attendant fears for their cultural identity, material privilege, and the possibility of revenge. It is for this reason that South African government spokesmen have declared that the practice of white supremacy can be defeated only by violent revolution. The most benign sharing of political power would depreciate relatively the present material situation of the low-paid white worker and of the Afrikaner farmer, who constitute the electoral basis of the Nationalist Party. The South African Government would brandish the *ultimate* goal of an integrated society as the *immediate* aim of a foreign intervention, and the apparently innocuous proposal for a conference as the opening of the floodgates.[1] To this call the Afrikaner Volk would rally as a man. They are not settlers, but a people; they may break, but will not bend. However reluctantly, the majority of the English-speaking South Africans will be obliged to make common cause. The degree of coercion necessary must therefore be sufficient, not to bring about the fall of the present Government only, but to oblige a whole dominant minority, more than three million strong, to abandon that position, and with it, the only way of life most of them—or their ancestors up to many generations—have ever known. As Dr Verwoerd expressed it recently:

> We will fight with our economic strength, if it is boycotts we face; and with our sons and daughters and ourselves, if it is force. For us it is a matter of life or suicide.

106. The second view is optimistic and less radical. It stresses first the division between Afrikaans- and English-speaking South Africans. In spite of political failure, the latter still control 99 per cent of the mining capital, 94 per cent of the industrial capital, 88 per cent of the finance capital, 75 per cent of the commercial capital. The great business concerns have nothing to gain and everything to lose from defying

[1] How accurate this interpretation is can be seen from ch. 4 of the report of the U.N. Expert Committee, which makes similar proposals for representative discussions. Not only is there envisaged a general amnesty, new elections and constituent assembly, but the principle of 'equality before the law of all persons regardless of race, creed or colour' (the Permanent Representative of Denmark to the United Nations) is stated to mean the abolition of laws such as the Native Land Act of 1913, the Native Trust and Land Act of 1936, the Group Areas Act, the Masters and Servants Act, the Industrial Conciliation Acts, the Mines and Works Amendment Act, the Native Building Workers Act, the Apprenticeship Act and the Native Labour Regulations, which reserve specific classes of work for whites only. Opposition is naturally increased by the idea of outside intervention, but when the U.N. Expert Committee suggests 'concerted international pressure' (para. 88), it is only being realistic, given that the whole proposal for a national convention rests upon the principle that the decisions themselves must be taken 'by the people of South Africa—*all* the people of South Africa—in free discussion' (para. 8).

economic sanctions. Some English-speaking South Africans, especially those who served in the world wars, would feel a terrible conflict of loyalties if Britain supported the United Nations in applying sanctions, and participated in the measures of enforcement such sanctions would require. Thirdly, there are uneasy consciences among many Afrikaners themselves. The Geyser heresy trial shocked many, for example. Lastly, when after Sharpeville world opinion was really stirred, and there was a withdrawal of capital, their reaction was not all defiance: voices were raised calling for a change of policy. Has the affluent society made the Afrikaner 'soft', less willing to fight than his Voortrekker ancestors whose deeds he celebrates every 16th December, is a question many ask in South Africa. Compliance would be yet more likely if the rest of the world threatened full sanctions. Above all, the apocalyptic alternative would lead a majority to see that compliance with the moral judgment of the world was the only sane course. As the U.N. Expert Committee puts it (paras. 39 and 131):

> We believe that the dangers are so great that there may yet be a desire, and consequently there may still be time, to avoid a vast and bloody collision. . . . If the threat is universal and complete, the imposition of sanctions might in fact become unnecessary. . . . What is now at issue is not the final outcome, but the question whether on the way the people of South Africa are to go through a long ordeal of blood and hate. If so, all Africa and the whole world must be involved. We believe that the course of reason and justice which we have advocated—a course which could be promptly and honourably accepted by all—offers the only way and the last chance of avoiding such a vast tragedy.

107. As to which of the two views may prove correct, everything could depend on the way in which the issues were presented. No more grievous disservice can be done to the hope of reconciliation than to present the issue as one of unconditional surrender, the imposition by the United Nations of immediate black majority rule over the whites, without there being any limit on the action of such a majority in the future. *If, on the contrary, the issue is put in the terms outlined in paras. 73-74 of this Report, with acceptance of a transition period, and subsequently community, as well as individual, rights ensured in a Bill of Rights underwritten by international guarantee, then everything could change.* The economic consequences for some sections of the white community could be counter-balanced by general economic expansion. The political sharing of power could find new expression in a South Africa welcomed back into the community of nations, and playing her rightful and leading role in the new Africa, for which her modern industrial society uniquely fits her. Once the initial fear of revenge has been

banished, why should a white South African fear his superior education and abilities will not ensure him a leading position in an integrated society? To those without faith in God's power to change even the most desperate situation, to mention this possibility may seem the hallmark of totally unreal idealism. But, unless the positive possibilities—which those who know South Africa recognize—are stressed, there is no outcome to be looked for other than the eventual conquest of the southern tip of Africa by the rest of the continent, at the cost of a sea of human bloodshed and suffering. As a leading article in *Die Burger* expressed it four years ago:

> History teaches us what power resides in movements that are imbued with the belief that time is on their side. And time, in super-abundance, is behind the black people, who are desirous of capturing political control in Africa.

Faced with the inevitable fate—as in Algeria—of ruling minorities who seek to retain everything, and so lose everything, reason adduces a powerful argument for seeking a third way. Christian understanding of history and knowledge of God's saving grace in our own lives means that we can never exclude such a change of heart as a practical possibility.

108. Whichever of the two interpretations is valid concerning the degree of coercion envisaged, it is no less necessary to examine whether economic sanctions could provide either, in relation to South Africa. The premise must be a United Nations decision, implemented by all member states. Otherwise, the cutting off of supplies by one country would simply mean their being supplied by another.[1] In particular, South Africa's nine main suppliers, which between them account for three-quarters of South Africa's external trade, would have to act together. These are: the United Kingdom (30 per cent), the U.S.A. (16·5 per cent), the Six (19·3 per cent)[2] and Japan (4 per cent). As the then South African Minister of External Affairs, Mr Eric Louw, expressed it in 1962, 'The nations not supporting sanctions absorb 79·6 per cent of South Africa's exports, and send her 63·7 per cent of her imports.' However, even assuming these powers jointly decided to reverse their present policy, there remains *the essential problem that total economic sanctions are a blunt and slow instrument of coercion*, as the historical lessons of blockade and siege would lead us to expect.

[1] A boycott of South African exports, though part of total sanctions, would simply be an indirect and slow means of cutting South African imports. A ban on sales to South Africa supposes that South Africa would stop exporting her goods, gold and services to the rest of the world.

[2] Of which Western Germany represents 10 per cent, France only 2·7 per cent. For the detailed break-down of the South African trade pattern, see Appendix XV, p. 136.

109. It is for this reason that partial sanctions are to be excluded.[1] The most widely canvassed proposal has been that of oil sanctions,[2] yet it may be shown that these would be entirely inadequate to coerce a resolute South African Government, major difficulty though they would cause. *The important point which the case of oil demonstrates is that no sanctions would be effective without a naval blockade. It also demonstrates the strength of the South African position to resist any form of sanctions.* To evaluate the vulnerability of South Africa to economic sanctions as such is therefore the next step.

110. Here in particular we are dependent on which of the two interpretations of the will to resist of the three million white South Africans is correct. To evaluate the absolute vulnerability of South Africa to total sanctions, one must assume the extreme case: a complete resolve to resist; a total embargo on all supplies, continuing until either the South African or the international will gives way. This position presents itself along the following lines.

111. Exports account for one-quarter of South Africa's gross domestic product, imports for one-fifth. These proportions indicate the severe damage to the South African economy which would occur in the event of total sanctions—but they do not by themselves indicate irresistible coercion. It must be assumed that, before sanctions became effective, there would be substantial stockpiling of all strategic materials, such as rubber, ball bearings and lubricants. Unlike other African countries, South Africa is self-sufficient in terms of iron, steel and coal. If the South African imports are analysed, they reveal that half consist in materials for industry, the remainder being divided roughly equally between consumer goods and capital equipment. It is the materials and equipment for industry which are the most significant. Apart from oil, the most vulnerable import categories are engineering and transport equipment (43 per cent imported) and chemicals (38 per cent). Textiles and clothing are imported in large quantities, but they are not strategic materials.

112. If it is assumed that the South African Government establishes rationing and puts the country on a war footing—as would most certainly be the case—these deficiencies would not be decisive. Capital equipment can be allowed to run down. The cessation of exports would permit a redistribution of internal production. As this would require time and major industrial surgery, unemployment would grow in the Reef, the Cape, and (particularly) in the Port Elizabeth area. Initially, mining production could be continued and stockpiled to prevent unemployment, and therefore unrest, reaching dangerous proportions. A proportion of the African labour force could be returned to subsis-

---

[1] Cp. U.N. Expert Committee's report, para. 108.
[2] See Appendix XVII, p. 144.

tence farming; others could be returned to their place of origin: Mozambique and the Protectorates. But South African industry would not be brought to a standstill. What would happen would be a heavy impact on the business community, on agriculture and the way of life of all white South Africans (particularly through severe petrol rationing). Luxury goods would be in immediate short supply. Shortages would increase in a range of engineering products. Maize would replace imported wheat in bread-making. So the list might be extended. *The important conclusion is that, given the will, the South African economy could continue on a siege basis for a period of several years. The only limiting factor would be the ability of the internal security forces to maintain law and order.*

113. This still leaves the question of how total economic sanctions could be imposed. The coastline of South Africa is 1,600 miles, and some forty vessels enter her ports every day. Angola and Mozambique, through which goods could be re-exported to South Africa, represent another 1,500 miles, with some twenty vessels entering their ports each day.[1] Given the huge areas of sea involved, only a full-scale naval blockade with task forces of fleet carriers,[2] equipped with planes using advanced radar, to direct warships towards approching merchantmen, would be effective (apart from submarine smuggling). The size of such task forces is daunting: five to seven fleet carriers, and perhaps fifty patrol vessels. The only powers which could mount such a force are those very Western powers which provide most of South Africa's imports. The U.S.A. has twenty-six fleet carriers in active service; Britain, four; France, three. Australia, Canada, the Netherlands and India have one each. The Soviet Union has none. The Cuban precedent suggests that the cost of maintaining such a blockade might be $150,000,000 per month, which would be a United Nations operation far larger than anything hitherto conceived. This reveals that *the whole concept presupposes the cold war to be suspended sufficiently for naval forces of this size to be withdrawn from their current assignments* (e.g. Borneo, or the American Sixth Fleet in the Mediterranean), and that the U.S.S.R. would contribute financially to such operations, which hitherto she has consistently refused to do. Above all, the whole operation would require to be mounted for a period, not of weeks or months, but perhaps years.[3]

114. At no point is the practical unreality of the proposal more apparent. If the assumption is correct that the South African Government has the will to sustain a total cessation of imports, and can main-

---

[1] A naval blockade of the major ports, which alone have oil unloading and storage facilities, might suffice in the case of oil sanctions, but not for other supplies.

[2] The task forces would have to reckon with there being no significant harbour within 2,000 miles of the Cape. Simonstown would be a hostile port. The airfields in Northern Rhodesia and Katanga are 1,500 miles to the north, and 500 miles from the sea.

[3] Approximate cost: $1,800,000,000 per year.

tain order internally, then a naval blockade would mean a *de facto* Soviet-American agreement to suspend the posture of the cold war in a significant degree for perhaps two years, in order to coerce three million recalcitrant white South Africans—rather less than the population of the City of Chicago, rather more than the population of the metropolitan area of Manchester. Concerning this, three things may be said. The first is that it gravely overestimates the importance South Africa has in the geo-political hierarchy of importance for either East or West.[1] The second is that, if the NATO powers really decided it was a strategic imperative to bring *apartheid* to an end—to avoid alienating the rest of Africa, to remove the incentive for an African attack on South Africa with Communist support, to retain Western control of the tip of Africa—then means would surely be found of so doing which did not involve the improbable posture of a sizable proportion of the total aircraft carrier resources of the West standing off the coast of Africa for a period of years. Assuming the balance of interests had been struck and ties of blood discounted, the real difficulty about direct action would be the Anglo-Saxon respect for the rule of law and the rights of a sovereign state.[2]

115. The third aspect that needs stressing is the curious ambivalence of thinking about the proposal for total sanctions. It seems to be assumed that, because *apartheid* has been denounced by the Soviet Union, it follows that she will wish to help the West bring it to an end. The one zone specifically excepted by the Soviet leaders from the *détente*, however, has been precisely those areas where uncostly Communist expansion may be looked for, because hunger and the desire for freedom act for the Soviet Union as did Marshal Winter in the struggle with Nazi Germany. It has been argued:

> The choice for the West will be between trying to prop up a racialist dictatorship and trying to wrest from the Communists the credit for bringing about its overthrow. If this choice is left too late, the latter possibility may no longer exist. If we do nothing, we are virtually ensuring that the Russians and the Chinese will be pushed

---

[1] *If* there were a U.S.–U.S.S.R. agreement about South Africa, it would be more likely to be one of mutual abstention, because their basic interest is to reduce, not create, areas of 'open-ended' conflict. China can neither provide troops in Africa nor ships to take them there.

[2] Cp. Article 51 of the United Nations Charter:
    Nothing in the present Charter shall impair the inherent right of individual . . . self-defence if an armed attack occurs against a Member of the United Nations.
 The Article was quoted by Mr Butler in the House of Commons as recently as 17th June, to justify the continued export of arms to S. Africa. As is pointed out (para. 116 below), the principal item at present being exported from the U.K. is the one weapon the S.A.A.F. would possess that could attack the capital ships in a blockading force: the Blackburn Buccaneer.

into the job themselves, and will become the heroes of three decades
to come of three continents—Latin America, Asia and Africa.[1]

Why should this prospect be thought unpleasing to the Soviet Union?
What *raison d'état* would lead her to support an operation undertaken
reluctantly by the West to retain Western influence at the tip of Africa?
Yet, without Soviet approval, the Security Council cannot act, and the
whole moral basis derived from a United Nations law-keeping operation
evaporates.[2] Indeed, the Soviet Union has a strong reason *not* to agree,
as it would involve a complete reversal of her previous position with
regard to the use of U.N. forces composed of troops from the major
powers.[3] Hitherto the Soviet representatives have consistently maintained that, as the special agreements referred to in Article 43 of the
Charter have not been concluded (owing to Soviet refusal so to do),
the Security Council cannot order the 'operation by air, sea or land'
provided for in Article 42. To assume that the Soviet Union would
readily be prepared to reverse her position is to assume much.[4]

116. This type of factual analysis is of moral value because it reveals the nature of the operation which is implied by the phrase 'economic sanctions'. In a message to the International Conference on Economic Sanctions against South Africa in April, Mr Harold Wilson wrote:

> The imposition of a trade boycott, including oil, is an act little
> short of war.

Blockade itself *is* an act of war in international law. The South African
Air Force would, for instance, be legally justified in attempting to sink
any blockading ships. The Buccaneers which the United Kingdom is
still intending to supply are specifically designed for such operations. A
blockade would also apply to the High Commission Territories, which
are in customs union with the Republic: measures of retortion against
them by South Africa would be legally defensible. *But the real sense
of the proposal lies in its frank recognition that economic sanctions—even
if enforced by blockade—would be ineffective. Swift results are required.
There would also have to be widespread internal disorder—or uprising—
at the same time,* brought about by mass unemployment and economic
breakdown, and aided by the resistance fighters at present being

---

[1] The *Observer*, 19th April 1964.
[2] The General Assembly can only recommend military sanctions under the
Uniting for Peace resolution if there exists an actual breach of the peace—not
a threat to the peace.
[3] Cp. Article 106. The U.K. and U.S. have contended that the powers of the
Security Council under Articles 41 and 42 are independent of the provisions of
Article 43.
[4] The Soviet note to Japan of 6th July 1964 envisaging a U.N. 'brush fire'
force composed of *non*-Security Council powers' troops is more akin to the
existing Scandinavian force, and does not invalidate the point about Soviet
approval of e.g. American forces being used in South Africa.

trained at Dar-es-Salaam who could be infiltrated into the territory of the Republic.

The new policy—we must face it—amounts to promoting a revolution.[1]

Indeed, unless this were the hypothesis, economic sanctions are not a realistic proposition to bring about the fall of the régime—always assuming the will of the white South Africans to resist to the end remains. Frank recognition of this is given when it is envisaged that a U.N. force would take over in South Africa in order to prevent Congo-type chaos, and the massacre of the white population after the Government could no longer control the mounting tide of disorder.

c. *The Legal Position*

117. In para. 93 it was stated that a condition for Christian approval of any action must be that it upheld the rule of law. The difficulty is that the present state of international law does not correspond to the moral realities of the world situation, and it is therefore only too easy to develop a legal case for non-intervention based ultimately on intangible national sovereignty. However, it must be recognized how tenuous in the present state of international law the legal arguments for sanctions are.

118. The basic arguments have been summarized as follows:

> The primary threat to peace is constituted by the South African Government's use of force against the majority of its own population. Secondary threats come from the massive build-up of South African armed forces, which menaces the independent countries of Africa, and from the hostile reactions of the African population within and beyond the borders of South Africa. . . . In so far as any attempt to bring effective pressure to bear on South Africa involves a risk of force being used—and this risk should be frankly noted—the prime responsibility for this situation rests not on those who are attempting to bring about a change, but on those who are ruling by violence.[2]

119. The first point to be noted is that, if a threat to the peace is established, then the 'domestic jurisdiction' argument from Article 2 (7) of the Charter fails, as it lays down:

> This principle shall not prejudice the application of enforcement measures under Chapter VII.

However, the 'threat to peace' itself, as set out in the quotation in the last paragraph, reveals itself to be that the internal acts of the South

[1] The *Observer*, 19th April 1964.
[2] Report of the Legal Commission of the International Conference on Economic Sanctions against South Africa, April 1964.

African Government are considered so provocative by South Africa's neighbours as to be *tantamount* to a threat to peace.

120. Many questions here pose themselves. In so far as there appears an overt preparedness for external aggression, it is from the Addis Ababa powers that South Africa might herself legally claim United Nations protection (South Africa's 'right to defend herself' is a basis invoked for the continued supply of arms from the United Kingdom). Secondly, while the Nuremberg trials indicate that racial oppression is internationally justiciable *ex post facto*, how far are the cases analogous, and if so, is this sufficient basis for prior international intervention? On examination, it will be seen that the basic case is in fact not legal, but political, namely that unless measures are taken now, 'the South African racial situation will lead to a crisis so bloody and so embittering to the population of South Africa that it will endanger the peace of the world';[1] that by failing to sanction interference our country is actively encouraging the continuance of racial oppression which, for safety's sake, or righteousness' sake, must be brought to an end. It is the case for prophylactic force based on the moral indignation of mankind.[2]

121. It is here that the legal truth is revealed: *it is less an issue of a threat to peace than of basic human rights*. Article 55 (*c*) of the Charter states the United Nations will:

> promote universal respect for and observation of human rights and fundamental freedoms for all, without distinction as to race, sex, language or religion.

To 'promote' is not a binding obligation by itself, but it must be read in conjunction with Article 56, which provides that:

> All members pledge themselves to take joint and separate action in co-operation with the Organization for the achievement of the purposes set forth in Article 55.

Together, these Articles impose direct responsibility upon *member* states (which would not be the case if South Africa left, or were expelled from the United Nations). But not only is there no binding force in the Universal Declaration of Human Rights, which seeks to spell out the implications of Article 55, but there are no sanctions laid down in the

---

[1] The *Observer*, 19th April 1964.

[2] A secondary but important issue is that a blockade, as an act of war in international law, comes under Article 42 of the U.N. Charter, but, as has been pointed out above (para. 115), Article 42 depends on the prior conclusion of the military agreements referred to in Article 43. However, the failure to conclude these agreements is probably no bar to a unanimous vote (i.e. of the permanent members) of the Security Council 'recommending' members to use military force. The Soviet note to Japan proposing a permanent U.N. force suggests the U.S.S.R. are now prepared to see military or economic sanctions being decided upon by the Security Council. This would be the first use in the history of the United Nations of Chapter VII of the Charter, under which Security Council recommendations are mandatory.

Charter for a breach of Article 56 (other than suspension under Article 5, or expulsion under Article 6 for persistent violations of the Charter). It is because the human rights provisions are not enforceable by sanctions that the threat to the peace argument has been invoked.

122. The international community is therefore faced with a call to develop human rights aspirations into supranational law enforced by military sanctions hitherto reserved for threats to the peace, breaches of the peace or acts of aggression. To phrase it thus is not entirely fair, in that what is sought is a remedy for an exceptional case where the breach of human rights on a race basis is elevated into a principle of state action, rather than the creation of a new system of supranational law. Nevertheless, it would represent an unprecedented increase in the legal claims of the world community upon sovereign states. In Europe some development in this sense has taken place with the supranational elements in the European Convention on Human Rights, above all in the sense that the rights are legally defined, and steps for enforcement provided. But that is within the comparatively tight and coherent West European community in a Convention ratified in the aftermath of a war against Nazism.[1] Can a yet more radical step be taken among states as disparate as those that compose the United Nations? There are breaches of human rights occurring every day in countries throughout the world. Is international intervention to be legalized in all these cases? It may be correct to argue that this is an extreme case, but where can the line be drawn? The best case for accepting the challenge has been made by Mr Peter Calvocoressi:

> The main reason why the prospect is alarming is that the criteria for such intervention are not defined, with the result that intervention could become widespread, indiscriminate and misplaced. But the remedy is not to refuse to intervene; it is to define the cases in which intervention is to be permitted. Definitions come by prescript and by practice, or, as we should say in domestic affairs, by legislation and by test cases. In international affairs there is little of either and a need for more. Good cases make good law, and the South African case is a good occasion to test, define and extend the rule of law in human affairs.

123. This is an argument that has much more appeal in Christian terms than the repeated statement of Afro-Asian spokesmen that, if the United Nations proves incapable of bringing remedy to the South African situation, it could lead to the disintegration of the United Nations itself. So, equally, could sanctions improvidently undertaken and demonstrated to be ineffective. Nor should the numerical representation of the Afro-Asian states in the General Assembly lead them to conceive

[1] And still unratified by France fourteen years after signature.

of the United Nations chiefly as an instrument for coercing the Western powers, which, in respect of South Africa, have both to take the measures and to bear the major consequences of their being taken. It is for this reason that *the moral basis of the action envisaged has to be clear, and to be more than the lesser of two evils.* The extension of the rule of law in terms of human rights could constitute such a basis.

D. *Conclusions*

124. Many of the arguments adduced in the preceding sections have related to the brutal facts of power politics. Unless these are taken into account, there can be no Christian judgment. This does not mean that Christian understanding of the real situation is limited by, or contained within, the power-political dimension.

125. The basic political premise is drastic action now to prevent yet more drastic action later, with the advantage that action now would mean under Western control; action later would mean the reverse. If the West continues to *promote apartheid* by continued investment and trade, the situation inside South Africa will become steadily worse, with increasing sabotage and murder being answered by an increasingly all-embracing police state. Outside South Africa, the buffer states will fall one by one: Angola, Mozambique, Southern Rhodesia. However long it takes, whatever their present military weakness or internal difficulties, eventually the other African states will mount a military assault on South Africa 'to liberate their oppressed brethren'. In terms of present military power such an attack is unthinkable; in any event, the logistics difficulties can hardly be overstressed. But these very difficulties—and certainly the likely initial defeats—would mean that Communist help would be sought. Indeed, it is likely to occur long before the phase of regular military operations, when 'freedom fighters' are infiltrated and it is sought to develop an Angola-type situation. In the long run it is difficult to conceive that the tip of Africa can defy the remainder of the continent, if its inhabitants are welded together in a crusade with a commitment as unrelenting as that of the Jews to their people in Nazi Germany. That is, unless the tip of the continent is a permanent bridgehead for other continents; which poses once again the basic choice for the United States of America and the United Kingdom. Put in terms of a cold weighing of strategic advantage, the balance might be held to be in favour of not driving Africa into the Communist-sympathizing bloc, at whatever cost to the three million white South Africans,[1] lest the balance of power be tipped against the West, and the security of *all* the free peoples be endangered. Translated into the policy of naval blockade, it would be seen as a choice between a race war now

---

[1] In such a perspective, to finance their total evacuation to Australia would be better than general massacre.

or a race war later, with the advantage that, by provoking a lesser (race) conflict now, it could prove less extensive, and above all would not get out of (Western) control. Taken to this point, if it were not for the respect of the rule of law among the Anglo-Saxon powers, the long-drawn-out nature of a naval blockade would make it military logic to invade South Africa, convene a constituent Assembly to establish a democratic constitution, and administer the whole area, preferably in the name of the United Nations, until those whites who had not taken advantage of assisted emigration were prepared to live under black majority rule with *their* human rights under U.N. guarantee.

126. Here we must take a stand. In such calculations the Christian Church has no place. The claim to be fighting race war reveals itself on inspection to be a move designed to spark it off, since the external blockade is likely to bring down the régime only if accompanied by internal insurrection. Nor is it acceptable to argue that, as the race war has already started (it began before 1910), violence is inevitable; that economic sanctions enforced by a blockade and followed by a U.N. administering authority will lead to far less bloodshed than will otherwise occur. This is to meet violence with more violence. Is such the characteristic witness of the Church to its Saviour Jesus Christ? This is to accept the theory of the '*jihad*', and to applaud the Crusades. Amid the shrill political voices already calling for violent action, the Christian witness is that violence can only beget violence, and that reconciliation cannot lie along that road. We must think less of the total situation than of the peculiar witness of the Church within it, which only the Church can or is likely to make. The first duty of the Church is to remind both protagonists that they are under judgment, that violence introduces a never-ending recession, of which neither justice nor love can be the outcome.

127. This basic Christian witness finds support in a cautious and pragmatic estimate of the facts of the situation. As long as an open race war has not been provoked, it has not occurred; the time thus gained can be used for a change of present *apartheid* policies. Once violence is resorted to, there can be no foretelling where it may end. The peculiar danger of the South African situation lies precisely in its 'open-ended' nature. The same is true of the problem posed: to change the whole structure and way of life of a society. Even if the régime should change, it would not remove race prejudice ingrained to the extent of a religion. A people that carried *apartheid* to the corpses in cemeteries will not abandon its tradition in a trice. Finally, governments are not structured so as to be able to deal with such problems. Distracted by crises all over the world—Cyprus, Laos, the Yemen, Borneo, Cuba, Israel—they are able only to deal with an immediate problem. Prophylactic action is foreign to their nature; allied to the intrinsic difficulty of the problem, it

follows they are likely to deal with it only when obliged to by external events. This may be unwise and costly, but this is how things will occur. Any realistic course of action must take such factors into account.

128. *If Christians cannot call for a naval blockade, followed by a U.N. expeditionary force, however, they have to face the challenge: what else do they propose?* Is the concern for love to exclude the concern for justice, or compassion for the Afrikaner to nullify compassion for the economic helots who are obliged to serve them?

129. This point has been eloquently put by Mr Peter Calvocoressi:

> If we condemn *apartheid* and sanctions equally roundly, what do we do then? Everything short of sanctions has been tried with but the least effect. *To oppose sanctions, which are the next and last resource, is to let* apartheid *be.*[1]

Archbishop Joost de Blank and Bishop Ambrose Reeves made the same point:

> Those who oppose sanctions must put forward some alternative method of bringing home to the South African Government the enormity of their policies.[2]

The incentive for so doing is heightened by a keen desire not to appear in any way to share the motives of some of those who invoke the evident legal and pragmatic arguments against sanctions in favour of the *status quo.*

130. A tentative answer may be sought along the following lines.

(i) *To cease encouraging* apartheid

(*a*) There is a complete opposition between the present position of actually supplying arms *to* South Africa, and *attacking* South Africa by an act of war (a naval blockade). *The sin of the present situation is that Great Britain is in fact encouraging* apartheid, and is therefore also morally guilty for the suffering it creates. In the eyes of many we appear as the country which could do most and in fact does least to end racial injustice in South Africa. A distinguished American Christian, Dr Henry P. van Dusen, relates a conversation with a member of the South African Government:

> So long as United States banks and business back us, we can go ahead![3]

How much more true this is of Britain, with an investment three times as great as America's in absolute terms, and ten times as great relative

---

[1] Letter to *The Times*, 21st April 1964.
[2] Letter to *The Times*, 22nd April, 1964.
[3] Letter to the *New York Times*, 6th September 1963.

to her total overseas investment.[1] The £60,000,000 of interest paid each year to British shareholders derives its particularly lucrative yield from the low wages paid to the black South African. In the mines the average wage for a white worker is $3,587, for a black worker $216 and his food. In Northern Rhodesia it is $810. *The first element in policy should be to move from a position of active support to a position of dissociation.*

(*b*) The criterion for deciding what action should be taken is to examine those present acts which the South African Government says give them the greatest encouragement to pursue *apartheid*. The first is the export of arms. Here a remedy can speedily be achieved (and will be in the event of a Labour Government). Investments present a more difficult problem. Existing investments cannot be recalled *en bloc*, though the Government could discourage or prohibit new capital investment in South Africa. All present repatriated South African dividends could be subjected to surtax, and the proceeds paid into a special fund for relief of the victims of *apartheid*.[2] Trade is particularly difficult because of Britain's balance of payments position, and the ready availability of foreign competitors for the South African market. As a small number of Western countries supply nearly three-quarters of South African imports, these states could decide to subject their exports to South Africa to a system of permissive licensing which would exclude strategic materials, and serve notice on the South African Government of the prospect of economic sanctions themselves. Emigration to South Africa could be the subject of special measures.[3] *Such steps, taken after careful working out of all their consequences, and with respect for the liberty of the subject, could merit Christian support in order to emphasize the complete dissociation of our country from a morally reprehensible policy.* At the same time, particularly in so far as they were the result of a collective decision by the key Western powers—a *sine qua non* in respect of export licensing, for example—they would probe the vaunted solidity of the white South African resolve to pursue *apartheid* to the last. *Such measures would be a logical continuation and development of the policy*

[1] 'Since the slump caused by world reaction to Sharpeville American investment in South Africa has risen by 25 per cent, and British investment has risen in a few years by more than £100,000,000 to a grand total of £1,000,000,000' (Report of the United Nations Expert Committee, para. 20). This total includes 'invisibles', which are not reflected in the dividend figure of £60 millions.

[2] To which widows and old age pensioners holding 'Kaffirs' would also be entitled to apply.

[3] Officially assisted and encouraged by the South African Government, white immigration has shown a sharp increase recently, rising to a figure of 30,000 last year. 10,000 came from the United Kingdom. At present South Africa is increasing her white population with immigrant settlers almost as fast as from a natural increase of her own white population. The current monthly figures are 4,000 per month from natural increase and 3,500 from immigrant settlers. Britain remains the greatest single source, there being 100 settlers of British stock to 10 from Germany and Greece, and 5 from the Netherlands, Portugal and Italy.

accepted by the Security Council, with Britain voting in favour, in Decem-
ber 1963, in recommending the prohibition of the export to South
Africa of certain categories of strategic materials, in particular equipment for the manufacture of weapons.

(c) They represent a logical half-way house between the present
policy of verbal denunciation[1] implemented by active indirect support
of *apartheid*, and a policy of active attack on South Africa because of
apartheid, which is what a naval blockade would mean. To proceed from
one extreme to the other would not only be impossible politically, but
would fail to give South Africa that last opportunity to change her racial
policy which it is in the general interest that she be given. It could be
that, in face of the prospect of full economic sanctions, her pocket will
prove more vulnerable than her heart, and the second interpretation of
the will to resist prove correct. Extreme measures can provoke only the
extreme reactions of resistance or surrender. As the latter is unlikely
initially, the result could only be to harden the situation, not to soften it.

(ii) *South-West Africa*

131. The judgment of the International Court of Justice will be
handed down in 1965. If this judgment is given against South Africa,
the matter will come before the Security Council. This is the kind of
situation that governments are structured to deal with, and they are
preparing to do so. Here is a field for potentially decisive action against
apartheid based on a clear international legal right, and not the tenuous
constructive doctrine of a threat to peace under Article 39. It will be
examined in greater detail in Section IX.

Taken together, the policies outlined in this and the preceding paragraph should constitute the first phase of policy, after which the situation would be reviewed in the light of events within, and around, South
Africa.

(iii) *Action by the Churches*

132. Both the preceding sections relate to the role of the British
Churches in influencing the policy of Her Majesty's Government.
There is also the peculiar role of the Churches in terms of the action
which they themselves may take.

133. First in priority is the intercession of the Churches in this
country, *with* the intercession of many Christians in South Africa, that
all white South Africans may be led to see the moral evil of *apartheid*,

---

[1] 'The policy of *apartheid* is evil, totally impracticable, and will lead eventually
but inevitably to disaster in South Africa itself. . . . The racial policies of the
Government of South Africa are entirely repugnant to my Government and to
the feelings and traditions of our people' (U.K. Permanent Representative in
the Security Council on 6th August 1963). Mr Patrick Wall, M.P., speaking for
the U.K. delegation in the Fourth Committee of the General Assembly on
12th November 1962, described *apartheid* as 'morally abominable, intellectually
grotesque and spiritually indefensible'.

and in particular that all members of the Dutch Reformed Churches may be led to see, as courageous men among them have already proclaimed, that *apartheid* is contrary to the teachings of Jesus Christ and has no warrant in Holy Scripture.

134. Second, the Churches must rebuild the bridges of communication broken down after Cottesloe, with a view to making renewed dialogue on the official level possible. At the Consultation on Race Relations in Africa held at Mindolo in June 1964, under the auspices of the World Council of Churches, no official N.G.K. or H.K. representatives were able to be present.

135. Thirdly, the Churches in Britain need to review the help they are giving to aid the victims of *apartheid* legislation, and in particular the dependants of political prisoners as well as of those imprisoned under the 90-day Detention Clause.[1] Such help falls under three heads:

  (i) Legal advice and defence;
  (ii) Family and personal relief;
  (iii) Help to those who take refuge in other countries.

With regard to (ii) and (iii) the proper channel in this country is the Christian Aid Department of the British Council of Churches. The World Council of Churches Division of Inter-Church Aid, Refugee and World Service has recently appealed to its related agencies (i.e. Christian Aid in the British Isles) for $1,000,000 for current emergencies in Africa, which includes substantial aid for South African refugees and for the dependants of prisoners and detainees. Christian Aid has sent a first contribution of £20,000. The Working Party believes the British Council of Churches should urge its member Churches to give all possible support to Christian Aid for the African Appeal. In addition, funds received by Christian Aid for (i), for which there is still pressing need, will be passed on to the appropriate organization.

IX. SOUTH-WEST AFRICA[2]

136. Throughout this Report[3] we have been deeply concerned about the ethics, legality and implications of concerning ourselves with another country's internal affairs. Article 2 (7) of the Charter is specific that '*nothing* contained in the Charter shall authorize the United Nations to intervene in matters which are essentially within the domestic jurisdiction of any state'. This scruple explains much of the legal argument examined above. The conclusion of the Working Party is that of Her Majesty's Government: *apartheid* has ceased to be a matter of purely domestic concern. But when it comes to taking remedial action, all the old objections again raise their heads. They have redoubled force pre-

---

[1] See Appendix XVIII for details, p. 148.
[2] See also Appendix XIX, p. 150.
[3] E.g. in para. 5 above.

cisely because the situation in South Africa itself is so deeply rooted in history that its remedy requires the reorientation of the whole structure of a society. It thus becomes an 'open-ended' problem, intractable to any political operation except drastic and enforced surgery, unless there is a change of heart among the dominant white minority.

137. South-West Africa is the reverse of this. It presents the following five main advantages to the world community now roused to end *apartheid*, yet still living with an inherited conflation of international law that no longer corresponds to the realities either of world unity or of world power.

    (i) Under certain circumstances the United Nations would have full legal right to intervene. Any action under Article 94 would necessarily rest on the firm legal basis of a court judgment and a delict committed.[1]

    (ii) The South-West African case has been so pleaded by South Africa before the International Court of Justice as to plead the whole case for *apartheid*. Its judicial condemnation in the case of South-West Africa would mean its implied condemnation in South Africa itself.

    (iii) The white population of South Africa would not die in the last dug-out for the sake of South-West Africa. The fact that in South-West Africa much larger proportionate participation of foreign capital investment has been encouraged suggests it would ultimately be regarded as expendable. The basic facts concerning South-West Africa lend weight to this view. The terrain is difficult, and requires enormous sums for development—over £120,000,000 is envisaged, for instance, in the Odendaal Commission's report. The proportion of white to black is much lower than in the Republic, being 1-7 instead of slightly over 1-4. Above all, the total number of white inhabitants is small—72,000 —and these are recent settlers[2] who *do* have another homeland.

    (iv) The judgment of the International Court of Justice is a definable event; it is a matter which may of right be placed on the agenda of the Security Council. It is therefore the kind of exercise with which governments are used to dealing. If remedy should be required, it is one that can be intellectually comprehended, and therefore a limit envisaged to its repercussions. None of this is true when the structure of the society of a historic nation state[3] is involved, as in South Africa itself. Yet because the issue is the same—*apartheid*—action in the former can justly be considered:

---

[1] Kelsen, *The Principles of International Law*, 1952, pp. 4–7.
[2] In 1918 they numbered only some 14,000.
[3] The Afrikaners arrived in South Africa only shortly after the Pilgrim Fathers arrived in North America.

and would be of immediate relevance to the latter. Indeed, it could constitute precisely that grave warning, that last chance for a peaceful solution, which all men of good will must seek, and hope that the dominant white majority in South Africa will heed.

(v) Successful United Nations action would demonstrate to the South African whites that the international community cannot be disregarded.

138. Before examining the position which may arise over the judgment of the International Court of Justice, however, it is necessary to review the findings of the sub-committee which the Working Party set up to study the South-West African situation as a whole.

139. The history of the question is set out in Appendix XIX. The essential point is that in 1918 South-West Africa was allotted to South Africa as a mandated territory, with permission to administer the territory, subject to safeguards, in the interests of the indigenous people. When, after the Second World War, the United Nations took over from the League of Nations, the existing mandates were changed into Trusteeship Agreements with the United Nations. This South Africa refused to accept in respect of South-West Africa, and she proceeded to a *de facto* annexation of the territory.

140. The following are the conclusions reached by the sub-committee concerning the methods by which South-West Africa has been administered since 1919, and the degree to which the terms of the original mandate have been observed:

(i) The indigenous peoples in South-West Africa have not been provided with such education as would fit them for independence and equality;

(ii) The indigenous peoples have not been settled on the land, nor has agricultural development been undertaken on their behalf, except to some extent in the 'reserves';

(iii) Industries in which the indigenous peoples can participate other than as ordinary labourers have not been developed;

(iv) A skilled or artisan class has not been created among the indigenous peoples;

(v) The political system which is being enforced in South-West Africa is designed to facilitate the economic exploitation of indigenous labour;

(vi) The territory is being administered for the direct benefit of its white population, most of whom have been settled in the territory subsequent to the granting of the mandate, and for the indirect material and strategic benefit of South Africa.

141. In our judgment, these facts justify the position taken up repeatedly by the General Assembly of the United Nations, that South

Africa has failed to carry out her duty under the provisions of the mandate, and that the policies of South Africa in the territory are in conflict with the requirements of both the mandate and the trusteeship systems.

142. This view will be put to the test when the International Court of Justice hands down its judgment in the case brought by Ethiopia and Liberia, the only African states formerly members of the League of Nations. The legal aspects of this matter are examined in Appendix XIX.

The Hypothesis of Resistance by South Africa

143. The essential point is that it is possible—indeed, governments are already actively preparing their position in anticipation of this[1]— that the following events may occur:

(i) The Court declares that South Africa must cease certain policies and repeal certain legislation in respect of South-West Africa which are incompatible with her international obligations;
(ii) South Africa refuses to comply;
(iii) The plaintiffs seek redress from the Security Council under the provisions of Article 94 (2) of the Charter.[2]

144. At this juncture Britain's full responsibility as a permanent member of the Security Council would be directly involved. Supposing for the sake of the hypothesis that there were unanimity in the Security Council, it might decide that the only way to give effect to the Court's judgment would be to appoint U.N. inspectors for the territory, or even remove the territory from South Africa's jurisdiction, placing it under direct U.N. trusteeship. This would then only bring the Security Council up against the twin problems already posed: in the event of South Africa refusing to accept such a decision,

(a) Would the Security Council be willing to seek to enforce its decision?
(b) If it so decided, by what means could it achieve this end?

145. This could reopen, via the case of South-West Africa, the whole discussion about sanctions already examined in relation to South Africa itself, on the assumption of South African recalcitrance, but with the vitally important differences outlined in paragraph 137 above. Even then, there would remain the physical problem of the means of coercion.

146. Given the clear legal basis in respect of South-West Africa, total sanctions might be more readily envisaged in United Nations— and Anglo-American—terms, but they would still be a blunt weapon, requiring years to be effective, providing the South African will to resist

---

[1] Cp. Appendix XIX, para. 24, concerning the consideration of a matter which is *sub judice*.
[2] For text see Appendix XIX, para. 27, p. 158.

was fundamental. The difference is that this will to resist is likely to be less adamant over South-West Africa than over South Africa. *Therefore even the brief application of sanctions—or the threat so to do by the Security Council—might well be sufficient to convince the South African Government that South-West Africa was not worth the economic disruption which sanctions would cause in South Africa herself, with all the wider implications of internal disorder.*

147. If this proved to be the case, then a wholly new position would arise concerning *apartheid* within South Africa.

   (i) The assumption of safe isolation would have been removed; the belief of the South African Government that it could defy the world with impunity would have been undermined.

  (ii) The long black frontier, though under U.N. control, would constitute a breach in the ring of buffer states around South Africa, and provide encouragement for the black South Africans.

Indeed, these very reasons are why South Africa would not concede control over South-West Africa easily. It is clear that South-West Africa in such a context would be seen by many as a stepping-stone, since South Africa would fear both infiltration from the north and that, if sanctions had been imposed to end *apartheid* in South-West Africa, they might later be applied to South Africa herself.

148. To harbour any such general intention would be to invalidate the main reason why the majority of the Working Party would be in favour of action in respect of South-West Africa, if it were based on a clear legal decision, namely that it could be treated as a specific operation which can provide the gravest warning to South Africa itself, and give the dominant white minority in that country a chance to alter the course of the *apartheid* policy without entering into the whole context of generalized coercion, with its grievous attendant risks and tenuous legal basis. *The majority of the Working Party believe that in certain circumstances South-West Africa may provide a unique opportunity for concerted United Nations action for limited ends, following which the proposal for a round-table conference would stand a much greater chance of acceptance.*

149. Any U.N. operation in respect of South-West Africa itself must have as its principal aim the welfare of the inhabitants. This would require special U.N. arrangements to raise the standard of living, education and economic activity of the indigenous peoples, the need for which is recognized in the Odendaal Report (though there one reason for it is no doubt in order to sweeten the pill of extending the principle of separate development into South-West Africa). The United Nations aim should be to give the peoples of South-West Africa independence, or, if it proves possible, a federal relationship with South Africa in pro-

spect of the racial policy of that country being changed so as to permit it. In any such context, the opposition and hostility of the indigenous people to the present South African Government must be taken into account.

150. For Britain the critical decision would be whether or not to veto a proposal in the Security Council which would seek to enforce the judgment of the International Court of Justice, in the event of the verdict being given for the applicants, and the defendants refusing to take the specific steps required by the judgment. The same decision would face the United States, in agreement with whom all measures should be concerted by Her Majesty's Government. To suggest that Britain might vote in favour but refuse to implement the decision itself would be morally unacceptable, and contrary to the provisions of the Charter. If Britain did use her veto, the whole principle of the rule of law and of the authority of the United Nations—perhaps its existence —would be called in question. But it is not solely for this negative reason that we believe that *Britain should in this case vote in favour of such measures as the Security Council may determine to uphold the rule of law in respect of the judgment of the International Court of Justice:* it is because such action by the United Nations would be in the best interests of the peoples of South-West Africa, of South Africa, of Great Britain and of the world.

151. In this event, Britain and the United States would have to envisage the flying in of United Nations officials to confer with the administration in South-West Africa, and later take over, South-West Africa would then become a trust territory under the direct U.N. administration pending her early independence.

The Hypothesis of Withdrawal

152. The more likely hypothesis is that South Africa will decide not to confront the world over South-West Africa, where her legal position is weak. Instead, she will decide—in the words of a member of the South African General Staff—to 'cut off the limb'. A first step in this direction was taken in deciding not to implement the Bantustan element in the Odendaal Commission Report in April 1964.[1] If the case goes against South Africa, and South Africa decides she cannot take the steps required of her, then long before the Security Council seriously considers action under Article 94, a kind of negotiation is likely to begin between South Africa and the United Nations, perhaps through the intermediary of the Anglo-Saxon powers. The kind of initial bargaining terms which it is understood the South African Government might put forward may be along the following lines:

---

[1] For details see Appendix XIX, para. 44.

(1) The permanent neutralization of South-West Africa, under the supervision of a Special Demilitarization Commission composed of representatives of the Allied powers of 1918 (i.e. including South Africa and Liberia, one defendant and one plaintiff state, excluding the U.S.S.R.);

(2) Recognition and continuation of Walvis Bay[1] as South African territory (to preserve the fishing industry);

(3) A period of at least two years for the withdrawal of the white farmers (and their sheep). These farmers to be given full compensation, at least 50 per cent of which should be paid for by the United Nations (perhaps £200,000,000);

(4) The Odendaal development projects being financed by the United Nations (£120,000,000).

Opening bargaining terms must be regarded as such; the significant fact is that there is preparedness to discuss terms of withdrawal at all.

153. More important than the morphology of this preparedness to withdraw is its likely effect. Estimates vary from the dramatic to the unnoticed. The truth probably lies in between. Such an event could provide an element of shock necessary to bring a sense of reality in the cocoon-like nature of present South African politics, as it would constitute a considerable blow to the prestige of those who seek to implement a policy of *apartheid*, and a decisive blow to the belief that South Africa can act permanently in defiance of the rest of the world. The South-West African frontier would be demilitarized: but it would have come 800 miles nearer. South-West Africa could still, therefore, mark a decisive point, even if the South African High Command decided to follow the Fabian tactics outlined above.

X. THE HIGH COMMISSION TERRITORIES

154. Time and time again in our study our thoughts have crossed the borders of South Africa to the neighbouring territories of Basutoland, Swaziland and Bechuanaland. These constitute an important complex problem in themselves, to which the British Council of Churches has already given attention. But they are not the specific subject of the present Report, in which we have been particularly charged to study the issue of sanctions and South-West Africa.

155. However, the issue of sanctions cannot be examined in terms of Britain's responsibilities without also examining the possible consequences for the High Commission Territories. For these reasons, an Appendix[2] has been prepared which summarizes the basic elements in the present situation.

---

[1] Walvis Bay has always been part of South Africa proper, not South-West Africa.
[2] See Appendix XX, p. 163.

156. Our essential concern must be for the welfare of the peoples in these territories. This should be to increase aid and investment by this country. It also means that Her Majesty's Government have a special responsibility in the United Nations to ensure that the world organization takes full account of the vulnerability of the three Territories to any measures of retortion which South Africa might take, in the event of sanctions being decided upon by the Security Council.

XI. CONCLUSIONS

157. It is fundamental to the revelation of God in Christ Jesus that:

There is neither Greek nor Jew, circumcision nor uncircumcision, barbarian, Scythian, bond nor free but Christ is all and in all.

It is for this reason that we are charged to 'put on a heart of compassion'. It is this compassion that has constrained us to seek to enter into the situation of those who have to bear the cross of reconciliation. Our concern is for all God's children in South Africa, of all races.

158. Reconciliation cannot be based on injustice, because injustice is a denial of love itself. Some situations contain a degree of evil and blasphemy[1] which makes their cleansing our required obligation. In the New Testament we read how our Lord cleansed the House of God, overthrowing the tables of the money-changers and using a scourge to drive out those who desecrated the Temple. Human beings are the temple of the Holy Spirit, and in South Africa they are being desecrated by a policy which erects inequality and exploitation into a principle, enshrines it in legal enactment, and for this blasphemy claims the warrant of Holy Scripture. The face of the oppressed African is the face of Jesus Christ.

159. The commitment of Christ's Church to the black peoples of South Africa is not in doubt. The witness of most of her leaders in South Africa has been outspoken and courageous, though hitherto few white Christians have been identified with their African brothers in their suffering. *This must come if the Church is to retain the allegiance of Africa.* It could prove that the attitude, practice and action of the Churches to-

---

[1] Cp. the statement of the Roman Catholic Bishops of South Africa in 1957:
  Apartheid is sometimes described as separate development, a term which suggests that under *apartheid* different races are given the opportunity of pursuing their respective and distinctive social and cultural evolutions. It is argued that only in this manner will these races be doing the will of God, lending themselves to the fulfilment of His providential designs. The contention sounds plausible as long as we overlook an important qualification, namely that separate development is subordinate to white supremacy. The white man makes himself the agent of God's will and the interpreter of His providence in assigning the range and determining the bounds of non-white development. One trembles at the blasphemy of thus attributing to God the offences against charity and justice that are *apartheid's* necessary accompaniment.

wards *apartheid* is, in the eyes of the Africans who are 270/275ths of the continent's population, the factor which controls the possibility of effective Christian witness in the future. Episcopal exhortations and the example given within the Church itself[1] no longer suffice in face of the choice now being presented between two kinds of state violence. In such a matter the Church has also to give its considered view as to the action the state should take, or be disloyal to Jesus Christ. It is our hope that the irrevocable choice, with its implications for the lives and suffering of so many, for the future witness of the Church in the whole of Africa, is not yet—that a third way is still open, that there is still some time for constructive action. *What is certain is that no action is in itself action: those who take no measures to end apartheid are guilty of its continuance.*

160. The peculiar responsibility of the Church has been referred to in paras 133-135. In no other grave international issue has the Church potentially a more decisive opportunity for witness, a witness of all those who love the Lord Jesus in all the Churches in South Africa, in Great Britain, in the Netherlands, in the United States, in France, and in all those states which share the decisions of the United Nations,[2] to be faithful to that same Lord. What others think of the possible role of the Churches is indicated in a document of the Security Council: the report of the Expert Committee delivered to the Secretary-General of the United Nations on 20th April 1964:

The conscience of the world has been stirred, and there is a recognition in world opinion that the South African problem is unique, demanding exceptional treatment. There is an international crisis of conscience; it arises from the fact that in South Africa there is a government professing to speak in the name of Christianity 'and the European race', which is the only government in the world which chooses as its guiding policy, not a striving to attain justice, equality and safeguards for human rights, but a determination to preserve privileges, defend discrimination and extend domina-

[1] More Christians in all the Churches of South Africa are coming to see that *de facto* segregation in their own worship and church life cuts the ground from beneath their witness to Jesus Christ, in particular vis-à-vis the state which only practises segregation *de jure*.

[2] Effective action vis-à-vis their governments may legitimately be expected of the National Council of Churches of Christ in the U.S.A., and of the French Protestant Federation in collaboration with the Conference of Cardinals and Bishops of France. South Africa was discussed at the joint meeting of the International Department of the British Council of Churches with the Committee of International Affairs of the French Protestant Federation which took place in London, 5th-7th December. Similar discussions with our colleagues in the Department of International Affairs, N.C.C.C.U.S.A., is being sought following the resolution adopted by the General Board of N.C.C.C.U.S.A. on 5th June 1964.

tion to such a degree that it amounts to the organization of a society on principles of slavery. In South Africa the denial of human rights and fundamental freedoms is openly pursued as an avowed policy. There are many in the Christian Churches and amongst those who can claim to speak for European civilization who can be expected to feel an exceptional responsibility in regard to developments in South Africa. Their influence in many ways and through many channels might be more effectively deployed' (para. 89).

The Churches in Britain no less than in South Africa are under judgment.

161. Is this the language of journalism or of history? We shrink instinctively from the misuse of adjectives like historic, from the dramatizing of one crisis among many, from over-simplifying the infinite complexity of issues which are not susceptible thereto, and distort the likely march of events to promote a given policy. On the key issue of the time-scale involved, we must pray that God will yet give us time to ensure by peaceful means that justice and reason prevail, and act in the belief that He will grant our request.[1] If this were not the case, and military operations were about to begin, the Church would be placed in its age-old, agonizing dilemma when faced with the arbitrament of force. Some Christians would feel the same doubt about praying for the victory of an African Liberation Army as they did when chaplains blessed the British Bomber Command 'planes taking part in thousand-bomber raids. Mercifully, this very perspective is evidence that we are not yet in such a position. There is time: but not much.

162. The fundamental point of departure must be the witness of the Church in the new Africa in the years until 2000 and far beyond. Both Protestant and Roman Churches recognize the fragility of much of the Christian implantation in Africa, weakness precisely because it is implantation and not indigenous. *If black Africa sees the white Church is more loyal to its whiteness than to the Cross, that white Church will have betrayed not only centuries of missionary sacrifice, but Jesus Christ Himself.* We would do well to hearken, therefore, to the words of one who has won the love and loyalty of Africans, Christians and non-Christians alike:

> I know that in these days a voice from Africa does not carry very far. There are too many voices, and England is perhaps tired of the clamour.
>
> But as a Christian pastor in the heart of the new Africa I am increasingly aware of a double failure on the part of Western Christen-

---

[1] For this reason, as well as evidence of growing points within the present situation, the Working Party cannot concur with the view expressed by the *Observer* on 21st June 1964: 'There is no imaginable peaceful solution.'

dom which seems to me to call for a renewed penitence and a renewed aspiration.

Because we are involved in the most revolutionary phase of Africa's history—the full realization of nationhood—we need faith: not in *our* conception of what African nationalism ought to look like and to be, but in God's plan and purpose within this marvellous moment of history. On the whole we fail to show such faith, and show instead a somewhat Pharisaic arrogance which cannot but alienate those who are building the new Africa.

But, even more deadly than this, we appear to be afraid of the revolutionary nature of our own Faith: a Faith which has given to the West its very belief in human dignity and freedom, and which has made a major contribution in Africa to this same fundamental belief. Yet now, when we should be proclaiming this from the house-tops, we seem to be suddenly fearful lest, by doing so, we may lose our status.

Christian opinion in Britain, in South Africa, in Southern Rhodesia, as it is expressed by the European—it is this by which so often Christianity itself is judged in the new post-colonial Africa. And although the voice of a Bishop Reeves or a Bishop de Blank may reach us comfortingly, we need rather more than this to match the present mood: we need the voice of the Christian Church itself. It is only such a voice which can drown the timidities and vacillations of diplomacy.[1]

Previous Decisions

163. What has the British Council of Churches said hitherto in this grievous issue of *apartheid*? In 1954, the British Council of Churches expressed its belief that:

> The policy of the South African Government as expressed in the Native Resettlement Act and the Bantu Education Act, whereby it is proposed to ensure the mental as well as the physical segregation of the Bantu 'in his own community', and to deny him any place 'in the European community above the level of certain forms of labour', is not only an offence against human rights, but also against the Divine Law as set forth in the Bible.

In 1960, the Council reaffirmed 'its whole-hearted support for the statement on race relations made by the Second Assembly of the World Council of Churches', which includes the declaration that:

> Segregation in all its forms is contrary to the Gospel, and is incompatible with the Christian doctrine of man and with the nature

[1] Letter from the Bishop of Masasi, the Rt Rev. Trevor Huddleston, C.R., *The Times*, 19th March 1964.

of the Church of Christ. The Assembly urges the Churches within its membership to renounce all forms of segregation or discrimination and to work for their abolition within their own life and within society.

In that year, our British Churches also took executive action within their own jurisdiction:

> The Council commends to the generosity of the members of its constituent Churches the plight of those at present suffering in South Africa through the policy of *apartheid*.
>
> The Council is glad that the Division of Inter-Church Aid and Service to Refugees of the World Council of Churches has already made resources available to meet this need, and offers its own Department of Inter-Church Aid and Refugee Service to receive gifts for this purpose. The Council further commends the Defence and Aid Fund of Christian Action as a channel of Christian generosity.

Conclusions of the Working Party

164. The Working Party unanimously agreed that the following conclusions should be emphasized in the light of the other judgments expressed in this Report:

(1) *Apartheid* is a blasphemy against the Holy Spirit.

(2) Its continuance threatens the peace of the world with the spectre of race war.

(3) There is still time to prevent this catastrophe.

(4) Nevertheless, it is not for the Churches of Jesus Christ to advocate a policy of total sanctions enforced by naval blockade, provoking the conditions of internal revolt which would justify —and require—a U.N. expeditionary force to prevent generalized chaos and massacre.

(5) The Churches must reject with equal firmness the present policy of Her Majesty's Government[1] of conniving at *apartheid*, by failure to bring to an end those actions which give encouragement to the Government of South Africa. In consequence, the Working Party believes there should be discussion with Her Majesty's Government concerning its scope for action in the sectors set out under I below.

[1] As of September 1964.

I. GOVERNMENTAL ACTION

A. SOUTH AFRICA

165. To dissociate the United Kingdom from *apartheid* in act as well as in word, and to cease all those things being done at this present by Her Majesty's Government or by British citizens which in South African eyes encourage that country's Government to pursue a policy which is, in the view of Her Majesty's Government, 'evil, impracticable and leading to disaster'. To request Her Majesty's Government to consider what measures it can take to this end. The following are given as *indications* of the kind of action the Working Party has in mind:

(a) Unilateral Measures

Arms

166. The immediate and total prohibition of the export to South Africa of any and all weapons; spare parts for weapons; and machinery, materials, plans or technical aid for producing weapons.

Privileges Dating from South African Membership of the Commonwealth

167. (a) The advantages of Commonwealth preference for South Africa to be ended.

(b) Holders of South African passports to require a visa.

Capital

168. (a) New capital investment in South Africa to be subjected to discretionary review, and if necessary, disallowance.

(b) Repatriated South African dividends to be subjected to surtax, and the differential between receipt from income tax and surtax to constitute a special *Fund for the Relief of the Victims of Apartheid*. Widows and Old Age Pensioners who depend on dividend income from South Africa for their livelihood to be eligible to apply for grants from this fund.

Emigration

169. Permanent emigration to be discouraged by:

(a) Imposing a specific '*apartheid* tax' on all air and ship tickets for travel to South Africa for purposes of emigration.

(b) Limiting to £10 per head money that can be expatriated to South Africa. Freezing of other individual capital assets in this country.

Conclusion

170. Such measures—unwelcome though they must be—could be taken unilaterally and be effective without the participation of other countries. If the latter choose to allow the further export of capital, it is

their investors who will lose it in the event of conflict. If they allow further emigration, it is their citizens who will be in danger. With trade it is different: this can be dealt with collectively or not at all.

(b) Collective Measures

171. The U.K. Government to approach the U.S. Government with a view to inviting the Six and Japan to set up a Special Licensing Committee for Trade with South Africa. Exports to South Africa valued above £5,000 f.o.b. to require the approval of this Committee, which would prohibit the export of strategic materials.

172. In the event of refusal or undue delay by South Africa's lesser trade partners, a joint Anglo-American Licensing Committee to be set up with similar functions.

173. *The difficulty and unwelcome character of such measures must be compared on the one hand with the catastrophe that will occur if South Africa continues with her present policies, and on the other, with the policy of total sanctions.*

174. The expert committee of the Security Council charged with examining measures against South Africa is to report not later than 28th February 1965. It could therefore be that next year the representative of Britain may have to cast his vote for or against United Nations sanctions. The measures indicated above approach the last point of peaceful action. If there is reluctance to implement collectively measures such as these, to consider the enforcement of sanctions is moonshine. The greater must include the less; the less could help make the greater unnecessary. It is in this hope and belief that the above illustrations have been given of the kind of action the Government might take. *The important point to establish is that it is the Government's pressing responsibility to review the whole scope of this country's relations with South Africa, and to decide what peaceful measures are required to stop Britain or her citizens giving encouragement to apartheid.*

175. The measures decided upon should be explained to the people of this country in an official statement setting out the Government's policy, and the reasons which led to its adoption.

B. SOUTH-WEST AFRICA

176. Britain should vote in favour of measures which the Security Council may determine to uphold the rule of law in respect of the forthcoming judgment of the International Court of Justice.

II. ACTION WITHIN THE REALM OF DECISION OF THE CHURCHES

177. Much of the emphasis in this Report has been political, because of the specific inclusion within our terms of reference of sanctions and

South-West Africa. In these matters, the Government will take account of Christian opinion, but it will decide independently. In other matters, within the fellowship of the Churches, it is the Churches which decide. Neither of these categories of action should be neglected because of the importance of the other. It is for this reason that the Report has stressed from the beginning the challenge for action by the Churches in this country in those spheres where they can implement their own decision. We see such action to be threefold.

178. (a) Developing Personal Contacts with the Churches in South Africa

Present casual contacts, chiefly through the presence in Britain of South African visitors, should be augmented through the planned encouragement of visits in both directions. Our various Churches should be extending invitations to laymen and ministers of all races and of all Churches.[1] Such visits would be mainly functional—to study youth work, industrial evangelism, ministerial training, to meet in Old Testament and New Testament seminars. In the reverse direction, and we are assured this would be welcome, a visit would be the occasion for discussion, in small representative groups, of common problems—juvenile delinquency, lay witness, church unity. In both cases, time spent in fewer places enables a visitor to know a few people well; a principle the more necessary where racial segregation makes social contacts less easy.

179. (b) Financial Aid for the Victims of Apartheid

The normal channel for aid is the Christian Aid Department of the British Council of Churches. This has already been described in paragraph 135, where an appeal to British Christians is commended. A more detailed account of the people who need our help is given in Appendix XVIII.

180. (c) Intercession

Prayer *for* must be prayer *with*. Our congregations are called to enter imaginatively into the situation of all the groups which make up South Africa, so that they may pray *with* them. The ministry of intercession has no boundaries: both those in 90-day detention and the police who interrogate them must be lifted up before the throne of God's mercy. For many in Britain this is the most real contact they can have with a country they have never visited; it is their point of immediate responsibility.

181. It is, however, upon Christians in South Africa that the main responsibility rests. United leadership by the Afrikaans- and English-

---

[1] For the most recent action proposed see Introduction to the Report, Section IV, p. 25.

speaking Churches—if translated into the attitudes and actions of their ordinary members—could make the decisive contribution to solving South Africa's grave political problems. For it is the total human approach that matters. There are still enormous reserves of good-will and preparedness to co-operate in freedom among the African majority. In this African Christians are outstanding. Nor are material resources lacking. South Africa could be—and by God's grace and in His time will be—a land greatly blessed in the freedom and prosperity of all her people.

5

APPENDICES

I · MEMBERSHIP OF THE SOUTH AFRICA WORKING PARTY

Chairman
The Rev. T. A. Beetham — Africa Secretary, Conference of British Missionary Societies; formerly Africa Secretary, Methodist Missionary Society, former service in Ghana

Secretary
N. H. Salter, Esq. — Executive Secretary, International Department, British Council of Churches

Members[1]
Sydney Bailey, Esq. — Formerly a representative of the Society of Friends at the United Nations

The Rev. N. C. Bernard — Africa Secretary, Foreign Mission Committee, Church of Scotland; former service in Nigeria, Nyasaland and Northern Rhodesia

Sir Frederick Bourne, K.C.S.I., C.I.E. — Formerly Governor of East Bengal

The Rt Rev. J. Boys — Director, South African Church Institute; formerly Bishop of Lebombo, Mozambique, lately Bishop of Kuruman

The Rev. C. H. Cleal — Secretary, Christian Citizenship Department, Baptist Union

Dr J. R. Gray — Lecturer, History Department, School of Oriental and African Studies

The Rev. A. F. Griffiths — Africa Secretary, London Missionary Society; former service in China

The Rev. T. Hawthorn — Secretary, United Bible Societies; formerly Johannesburg Secretary, British and Foreign Bible Society

[1] Not all the members were able to attend all meetings, so that individuals must not be considered as necessarily accepting every expression of opinion in the Report, though all have contributed to the final text. A deep debt of gratitude is owed to them for having given so generously of their time and experience.

G

K. R. Johnstone, Esq., C.B., C.M.G.	Chairman, International Department, British Council of Churches; formerly Deputy Director, British Council, and a Minister in H.M. Foreign Service
Canon J. S. Kingsnorth	General Secretary, Universities' Mission to Central Africa; former service in Northern Rhodesia
J. T. S. Lewis, Esq.	Secretary, the Capricorn Africa Trust
P. Mason, Esq., C.I.E., O.B.E.	Director, Institute of Race Relations
The Rev. H. O. Morton	Secretary for East and Central Africa, Methodist Missionary Society; formerly S.C.M. Secretary, Britain and India
Professor R. Niblett	Dean of the Institute of Education, University of London
Dr R. Oliver	Professor, History Department, School of Oriental and African Studies
The Rev. R. K. Orchard	London Secretary, Division of World Mission and Evangelism, World Council of Churches
P. Radley, Esq.	Society of Friends; former service in South Africa
The Rev. E. Rogers	General Secretary, Department of Christian Citizenship, Methodist Church
Lt Commissioner H. Westcott	Director, Social Welfare Service of the Salvation Army; former service in South Africa

Consultants

The Rt Rev. Dr Joost de Blank	Canon of Westminster Abbey (lately Archbishop of Cape Town)
The Rev. A. R. Booth	London Secretary, Commission of the Churches on International Affairs
The Rev. J. R. Gray	Conveyor of the Church and Nation Committee, Church of Scotland
Sir John Maud, G.C.B.	The Master, University College, Oxford (lately H.M. Ambassador to South Africa, and High Commissioner for the Protectorates)
The Rt Rev. Dr R. P. Wilson	Bishop of Chichester

Roman Catholic Observer

The Very Rev. Father Gerard Meath, O.P.	Prior Provincial

Adviser for Economic Questions
H. Latimer, Esq.
Adviser for Strategic Questions
N. Brown, Esq.

II · MEETINGS OF THE WORKING PARTY

1. Initially, the Working Party held meetings on 21st November, 5th and 18th December 1963, 7th and 13th January, and 12th February 1964. An introductory paper prepared by the Chairman formed the basis of study and discussion. The following addressed the Working Party and answered questions: Professor C. A. W. Manning, of the South Africa Society, at the suggestion of South Africa House; Mr Oliver Tambo, Deputy Leader of the African National Congress; the Rev. B. H. M. Brown, Secretary of the Christian Council of South Africa; the Hon. E. A. Gross, O.B.E., Chairman of the Department of International Affairs of the National Council of the Churches of Christ in the U.S.A., and legal representative of the applicants in the case of South-West Africa at the International Court of Justice. The introductory paper served as a basis for preliminary correspondence with several Christian leaders in Africa.

2. The Working Party then adjourned, in order to be able to take into account the following elements:

(1) The authoritative study on *The Church and Race Relations in South Africa*, published under the auspices of the South African Institute of Race Relations in July 1964.
(2) *The report of the Secretary-General of the United Nations to the Security Council in pursuance of Resolution S/5471, adopted by the Security Council on 4th December* 1963. This was published on 20th April and debated in the Security Council in June 1964.[1]
(3) The papers of the '*International Conference on Economic Sanctions against South Africa*', held in London in April 1964.

3. Above all, after the initial meetings, the essential need was for direct contact with the Churches—all the Churches—in South Africa itself. Some of our number have been deeply committed within the life of South Africa in the past, but as a group of the British Council of Churches we have by definition both the limitations and the advantages of those who can only see at a distance the situation they attempt to describe. It was therefore of the greatest value that, with the generous assistance of a Trust in the United Kingdom, the Chairman and Secretary of the Working Party were able to spend several weeks

[1] See Resolution S/5773, adopted 18th June 1964.

in South Africa in May-June, at the invitation of the Christian Council of South Africa. Initially, they attended the Biennial Conference of the C.C.S.A. and then a special National Conference on the theme 'The New Dimensions of Mission for South Africa Today'. Then there followed an intensive visit to the major cities of the Republic, the Transkei, the Reef and other areas, with conferences with church leaders and others representing all points of view, except the African opposition, which is legally proscribed, and thus could not be contacted (e.g. Chief Luthuli, the leader of the African National Congress). A consultant of the Working Party, the Rev. Alan Booth, also visited South Africa, prior to being present at the Conference on Race Relations in Southern Africa, held under the auspices of the World Council of Churches at Mindolo in June 1964, which was attended by Christian leaders from many parts of Africa.

4. The Chairman and Secretary wish to express their deep gratitude to all the South Africans they met, for the right hand of Christian fellowship which they so generously extended. To pray with so many fellow Christians has been an enriching experience to us both personally.

III · EXTRACTS FROM A LETTER WRITTEN BY THE REV. DR MARTIN LUTHER KING JR

This letter was written on 16th April 1963 in response to a statement made by eight clergymen (including a Rabbi, one Episcopal, one Roman Catholic and two Methodist bishops), calling the Birmingham demonstrations 'unwise and untimely'.

'. . . You deplore the demonstrations that are presently taking place in Birmingham. But I am sorry that your statement did not express a similar concern for the conditions that brought the demonstrations into being. . . . It is unfortunate that so-called demonstrations are taking place in Birmingham at this time, but I would say that it is even more unfortunate that the white power structure of this city left the negro community with no other alternative. . . .

'My friends, I must say to you that we have not made a single gain in civil rights without determined legal and non-violent pressure. History is the long and tragic story of the fact that privileged groups seldom give up their unjust posture. . . . . We know through painful experience that freedom is never voluntarily given by the oppressor; it must be demanded by the oppressed.

'Frankly, I have never yet engaged in a direct-action movement that was "well-timed", according to the timetable of those who have not suffered unduly from the disease of segregation. For years now I have heard the word "wait". It rings in the ear of every negro with a piercing familiarity. This "wait" has always meant "never". . . . We must come to see with the distinguished jurist of yesterday that "justice too long delayed is justice denied". We have waited more than 340 years for our constitutional and God-given rights. The nations of Asia and Africa are moving with jet-like speed toward the goal of political independence, and we still creep at horse-and-buggy pace toward the gaining of a cup of coffee at a lunch counter.

'I guess it is easy for those who have never felt the stinging darts of segregation to say "wait". But . . . when you suddenly find your tongue twisted . . . as you seek to explain to your six-year-old daughter why she can't go to the public amusement park that has just been advertised on television, and see tears welling up when she is told that Funtown is closed to coloured children, and see the depressing clouds of inferiority begin to form in her little mental sky, and see her begin to distort her personality by unconsciously developing a bitterness toward white people; when you have to concoct an answer for a five-year-old son asking, "Daddy, why do white people treat coloured people so mean?"; when you take a cross-country drive and find it necessary to sleep night after night in the uncomfortable corners of your automobile because no motel will accept you; when you are humiliated day in and day out by nagging signs reading "white" men and "coloured"; when your first name becomes "nigger" and your middle name becomes "boy" (however old you are) and your last name becomes "John", and when your wife and mother are never given the respected title "Mrs"; when you are harried by day and haunted by night by the fact that you are a negro, living constantly at tip-toe stance, never quite knowing what to expect next, and plagued with inner fears and outer resentments; when you are forever fighting a degenerating sense of "nobodiness"—then you will understand why we find it difficult to wait. There comes a time when the cup of endurance runs over, and men are no longer willing to be plunged into an abyss of injustice where they experience the bleakness of corroding despair. I hope, sirs, you can understand our legitimate and unavoidable impatience. . . .'

IV · STATISTICS OF POPULATION AND RELIGIOUS AFFILIATION

I. POPULATION

Year	White	Coloured	Asian	African	Total
1951 census	2,641,689	1,103,016	366,664	8,560,083	12,671,452
1960 census	3,088,492	1,509,258	477,125	10,907,789	15,841,128
% increase	16%	35%	30%	26%	25%
1961 official estimate	3,106,000	1,522,000	487,000	11,007,000	16,122,000

African: Major Groups 1960

Xhosa	3,134,265
Zulu	2,788,415
Bapedi	1,188,859
Sotho	1,156,436
Tswana	886,240
Shangaan	518,775
Smaller Bantu units	1,134,819

II. RELIGIOUS AFFILIATION[1]
a. BY RACES

Church	White	Coloured	Asian	African	Total
Nederduits Gereformeerde	1,326,344	442,944	519	556,898	2,326,705
Gereformeerde	101,470	7,292	—	—	108,762
Nederduits Hervormde	190,342	3,746	—	—	194,088
Total D.R.C.	1,618,156	453,982	519	556,898	2,629,555
Anglican	389,859	268,620	4,900	748,135	1,411,514
Methodist	269,825	117,903	2,019	1,313,129	1,702,876
Presbyterian	110,873	7,545	346	204,585	323,349
Congregational	16,656	137,358	188	135,167	289,369
Lutheran	33,631	73,457	—	539,213	646,301
Total[2]	820,844	604,783	7,453	2,940,229	4,373,409
Roman Catholic	192,799	119,845	10,277	760,607	1,083,528
Apostolic	107,700	69,638	954	304,583	482,875
Bantu separatist Churches	—	—	—	2,188,303	2,188,303
Other Christian	166,098	132,225	15,076	507,567	820,966
Jewish	116,066	—	—	—	116,066
Islam	—	93,256	98,490	—	191,746
Hindu	—	—	310,839	—	310,839
Other and unspecified	66,829	35,429	33,517	3,649,602	3,785,377
Grand total	3,088,492	1,509,258	477,125	10,907,789	15,982,664

[1] Source: *6th Report of the Population Census* (1960), Pretoria, November 1963.
[2] I.e. of the main member Churches of the Christian Council of South Africa.

b. BY PROVINCES

CHURCH	PROVINCE				TOTAL
	Cape	Transvaal	Natal	Orange Free State	
Nederduits Gereformeerde	1,020,983	815,630	89,442	400,650	2,326,705
Gereformeerde	17,847	73,981	2,916	14,018	108,762
Nederduits Hervormde	11,302	167,983	5,319	9,484	194,088
Total D.R.C.	1,050,132	1,057,594	97,677	424,152	2,629,555
Anglican	650,520	446,254	222,750	91,990	1,411,514
Methodist	827,198	441,642	226,371	207,665	1,702,876
Presbyterian	136,024	101,120	60,865	25,340	323,349
Congregational	227,120	32,910	20,919	8,420	289,369
Lutheran	119,522	379,716	129,278	17,785	646,301
Total	1,960,384	1,401,642	660,183	351,200	4,373,409
Roman Catholic	288,376	361,728	306,492	126,932	1,083,528
Apostolic	114,185	247,289	35,056	86,345	482,875
Bantu Separatist Churches	478,594	1,030,853	495,747	183,109	2,188,303
Other Christian	242,936	400,666	114,801	62,563	820,966
Jewish	32,389	74,221	6,266	3,190	116,066
Islam	89,082	42,707	58,957	—	191,746
Hindu	4,852	23,190	282,797	—	310,839
Other and unspecified	1,081,790	1,633,587	920,946	149,054	3,785,377
Grand total	5,342,720	6,273,477	2,979,922	1,386,545	15,982,664

V · THE 'CIVILIZED LABOUR POLICY'

In a circular (No. 5 of 1924), the Prime Minister defined 'civilized labour' as 'the labour rendered by persons whose standard of living conforms to the standard generally recognized as tolerable from the usual European standpoint', while 'uncivilized labour' was defined as that 'rendered by persons whose aim is restricted to the bare requirements of the necessities of life as understood among barbarous peoples'.

This also involved the employment of 'civilized labourers' at rates above those generally prevailing for unskilled labour. It has been implemented through the Wage, Industrial Conciliation and Apprenticeship Acts. In certain occupations (notably those managed by the Government, such as the railways), the effect has been that no African can be employed if a European wants his job.

Examples of recent Determinations by industrial tribunals are as follows:[1]

[1] Source: South African Institute of Race Relations, *Annual Survey* of race relations in South Africa, 1962.

Determinations in force at the end of 1961

No. 2, 1957, reserving for whites the driving of motor transport vehicles in the Durban municipal cleansing department;

No. 4, 1958, reserving for whites the posts of firemen and traffic policemen above the rank of constable in the Cape Town area, and placing restrictions there on the employment of coloured ambulance drivers and attendants and traffic constables;

No. 5, 1959, reserving for whites skilled work in the building industry in urban areas of the Transvaal and Free State other than in African townships (as is mentioned, certain exemptions have been granted);

No. 8, 1960, for the clothing industry. This is a complicated measure, the object of which is to prevent the percentage of whites employed by any employer, or of whites and coloureds together, from falling below the percentage that obtained at set dates.

Determinations published in 1962

No. 9.   During 1961 the Town Council of Springs decided to use lorries instead of mule-carts for transporting rubbish, refuse and night-soil, and to employ African drivers. As objections were lodged with the Department of Labour, an investigation by the Industrial Tribunal was ordered, and the Government then published Determination No. 9, which states that the work of driving these vehicles in the industrial areas or white suburbs of Springs must be reserved for whites. It was reported (*Rand Daily Mail*, 26th February) that, as a result, twelve Africans were replaced by white drivers.

No. 10.   Following a dispute between the City Tramways Company in the Western Cape and the Tramway and Omnibus Workers' Union over the employment of coloured drivers and conductors, Determination No. 10 was gazetted. This provides that on not less than 24 days in any month, at least 84 per cent of the drivers and conductors employed by the company must be white persons.

No. 11.   Complaints were received by the Department about the increasing extent to which Africans were being employed as drivers on the Free State Goldfields. Determination No. 11 laid down that in certain industries in this area the drivers of vehicles of an unladen weight of 10,000 lb. or more must be white persons. The industries concerned are cement products, meat, mineral water manufacturing, quarrying, brick-making, sale of sand, stone-crushing and the transportation of goods.

No. 12. Determination No. 12 relates to the wholesale meat trade on the Witwatersrand and in Pretoria. It reserves for whites various skilled types of work, including the driving of motor vehicles of an unladen weight of 10,000 lb. or more.

Investigations in Progress

Four types of investigations have been referred to the Industrial Tribunal. Firstly, it has been directed to investigate whether measures are desirable to protect whites against inter-racial competition in:

(*a*) the building industry in Natal and the Cape;
(*b*) the trade of barman in the chief towns of Natal.

Secondly, it is investigating whether measures are desirable to protect whites and coloureds against inter-racial competition in:

(*a*) the motor assembly industry;
(*b*) the operating of machinery used for road construction, levelling of ground, or removal of earth in the Transvaal, Free State or Natal.

Thirdly, the Tribunal is examining the desirability of measures to safeguard employees generally against inter-racial competition in:

(*a*) motor transport driving in Durban;
(*b*) the footwear industry;
(*c*) the furniture industry.

And finally, it is considering whether measures should be taken to protect coloured and Indian workers against African competition in:

(*a*) the laundry, dry cleaning and dyeing trade in the Western Cape and Natal;
(*b*) the liquor and catering trade in the Western Cape and Natal;
(*c*) occupations in private hotels and boarding houses in the Western Cape and Natal.

VI · BANTU EDUCATION

The Bantu Education Act of 1953 has now been in operation for ten years and a first attempt to assess its effects has been made in two publications of the South African Institute of Race Relations.[1]

The Act implements the Eiselen Commission on Native Education whose main terms of reference were:

(*a*) The formulation of the principles and aims of education for Natives as an independent race, in which their past and present,

[1] Muriel Hurrell, *A Decade of Bantu Education*; Nathan Hurwitz, *The Economics of Bantu Education in South Africa*.

their inherent racial qualities, their distinctive characteristics and aptitude, and their needs under ever-changing social conditions are taken into consideration.

(b) The extent to which the existing primary, secondary and vocational education system for Natives and the training of Native teachers should be modified in respect of the content and form of syllabuses, in order to conform to the proposed principles and aims, and to prepare Natives more effectively for their future occupations.

(c) The organization and administration of the various branches of Native education.

(d) The basis on which such education should be financed.

The South African Government was seeking to do what every other African government has done in recent years: to take stock of its educational policy, effect greater co-ordination and supervision of a dual system of church and government education with increasing local government involvement, plan for large increases in enrolment, and initiate an African-relatedness[1] to the basic principles and syllabuses of the curriculum.

In the rest of Africa, apart from Southern Rhodesia and the Portuguese territories, such decisions have been made by Africans, after consultation with overseas experts. It is they who have decided on the phasing of any transfer of management from Church to local government; it is they who have viewed the whole economy of their country and decided on the extent and content of education, and in particular what is to be the relation within it of African and European culture. In South Africa this decision has been taken by a white government, and within the context of exclusive separate development. It is these two factors which vitiate in African eyes an approach to an African basis for education which in other countries in the continent is accepted as desirable policy.

The framework of the system is avowedly one of separation. This is the reason why, unlike countries such as Ghana and Nigeria, South Africa has eliminated Church partnership in African education completely.[2] As Dr Verwoerd said at the time, 'Native Education should be controlled in such a way that it should be in accord with the policy of the

---

[1] What elsewhere is called the 'African personality' or 'négritude'.

[2] The Act makes provision for independent church schools if financed without government grant, but administrative regulations have made the continued existence of such schools increasingly difficult. For example, courses at church teacher-training colleges are not now recognized as qualifying for teaching in state and community schools; church school enrolment is now limited to members or children of members of the particular Church; 'registration' of church schools may be, and has been, refused on the annual re-application without reason given, and no school, however thriving, knows when its next application may be refused.

State. . . . Good racial relations cannot exist when the education is given under the control of people who create wrong expectations on the part of the Native himself. . . . (Racial relations) cannot improve if the result of Native education is the creation of frustrated people. Education must train and teach people in accordance with their opportunities in life, according to the sphere in which they live.' In 1959 the Minister of Bantu Education, Mr W. A. Maree, said, 'The paramount principle in the education of the (African) child in the urban areas must be just as it is in the Reserves, that we must try to retain the child as a child of his own national community, because it is the basic principle of Bantu education in general that our aim is to keep the Bantu child a Bantu child. . . . The Bantu must be so educated that they do not want to become imitators but that they will want to remain essentially Bantu.'

This conception of education for the African population has been continually criticized by Africans themselves as well as by members of the other communities. A national conference convened by the Institute of Race Relations in 1952 said, 'While accepting the fact that Africans are ethnologically a separate race, the Conference does not consider that they are a community unrelated to the rest of South Africa. It believes that Africans are not culturally, economically or politically independent, but that they are an integral part of South African society.'

To what extent have the aims of the Bantu Education Act been achieved, and what has been the effect in African schools and colleges?

Enrolment

The number of children attending school has increased rapidly, as it has throughout the continent. From 1955 to 1962 the total increased from 1,005,222 to 1,678, 388, as the following table shows:

CLASS	1955	1962
Sub. A	282,910	426,827
Sub. B	183,617	306,375
St. I	151,144	268,278
St. II	113,499	203,792
St. III	90,948	153,688
St. IV	66,101	112,103
St. V	47,353	85,466
St. VI	34,667	71,738
Total Primary	970,239	1,628,267
Form I	16,122	21,730
Form II	9,879	14,594
Form III	6,915	10,823
Total Junior Secondary	32,916	47,147
Form IV	1,393	2,006
Form V	674	968
Total Senior Secondary	2,067	2,974
COMBINED TOTALS	1,005,222	1,678,388

The large increase in the two sub-standards has only been possible by adopting a device which pertains also in some schools in West Africa, viz. by one teacher teaching two sets of children in succession in half-day sessions. At the same time, the number of pupils allowed in a class has been increased to 50. Most 'infants' teachers, therefore, teach 100 pupils, 50 from, say, 8-11, and another 50 from 11.30-2.30.

It will be seen from the table that of the 200,000 children known to have enrolled in Sub. A in 1950, only 968 reached Form V in the Secondary School thirteen years later. Of these 968 secondary pupils, 894 sat for Matriculation and 362 passed, only 4 in the first class.

Control

School Boards or Committees have been established for individual schools or groups of schools. No white members are allowed to serve on them, nor may teachers or wives of teachers. In rural areas, this means that a majority of the Committee may themselves be non-literate. There have been a number of cases of dismissal of teachers by these committees without any clear cause.

Buildings

In 1954, most Churches decided to rent their school buildings to the Government; the amount of rent they received enabled them to keep the buildings in adequate repair. It was announced during 1961 that all leases contracted between the Bantu Education Department and the Churches would terminate at the end of the year; new leases would have to be contracted with the local school boards. These boards have no money to pay the rent, and very few rents have, in fact, been received by the Churches since 1961. Since they are not prepared to eject the school children and cannot see the premises go into complete disrepair, they find themselves forced to find the money necessary for the upkeep and maintenance of the buildings.

Finance

In 1925 an Education Act introduced for the first time the principle that the cost of any increase in African education must be met from their direct taxation and not from the Consolidated Revenue of the country. This principle was partly rescinded in 1945, when Estimates for African Education were made presentable to Parliament and a vote allowed from general funds for any deficit. In 1955, however, the Bantu Education Act reversed this trend. A fixed sum was laid down as the annual contribution from Consolidated Revenue, £6,500,000. All expenditure beyond that, however much the demand for African education grew, must be met from African direct taxation. This sum now amounts to £3,900,000; this together with the £6,500,000 General Revenue and with certain miscellaneous school income makes up a total budget of £10,765,000. This has to cover all expenditure on African education apart from the salaries of the Senior Administrators, the cost of the University Colleges, and special schools for the handicapped.

The only figures available for a comparison of the net annual costs per pupil in other communities refer to the Cape in 1960-61. For white children the figure was £72 5s; for Coloured, £29 10s. In the same year the figure for Africans throughout the country was £6 5s.

The 1963-64 Estimates for African education for an enrolment greater than the figures for 1962 quoted above include the following items: School feeding, £25,000; text-books for pupils, £3,850; grants to school libraries, £1,400; night and continuation classes, £500 (against £22,000 for this item in 1955-56).

Considerable burdens fall on parents for expenditure other than uniform: writing materials, exercise books, etc; private subscriptions to make possible more teachers than the State allocates; levies for school buildings. An estimate for the year 1960-61 puts the African parents' direct contribution to education as:

£2,729,516	in direct taxation
57,112	towards erection of buildings
100,000	contributed towards salaries of teachers
1,430,316	special school fees, materials, etc.
£4,316,944	against the £6,500,000 from Central Revenue.

Future expansion and improvement of African education, therefore, depends on the ability of the African community to increase its own contribution, i.e. it must wait on the increase in the pay packets of the poorest section of the community, whose wage level is rising more slowly compared with the cost of living than any other section.

Language in School

The mother tongue is now the medium of instruction in the Primary School and is to become so in the Junior Secondary School. Afrikaans and English are taught as second languages from the beginning of the Primary School. Where it is not yet possible to provide textbooks in the mother tongue for all subjects taught in the junior secondary school, half of the subjects not taught in the mother tongue must be taught in Afrikaans and the other half in English. This is a greater handicap than that for children in other parts of Africa, where there is only one second language in the Primary School, French or English, and where the mother tongue ceases to be the medium of instruction after three or four years' schooling.[1]

[1] In a farm school visited recently, St. II children who had received their first two years' schooling in the double-classes already described, and had then been taught in St. I and II simultaneously by one teacher (sixty children in one classroom), read to the visitor successively from their Tswana, Afrikaans and English readers. Is it surprising that the reading was somewhat 'wooden'?

School Feeding

The Government vote for school feeding in African schools in 1949 stood at £870,000. This was severely cut that year, thus excluding some 285,000 African children from benefit. In 1956, Bantu school boards were given the offer of transferring the school feeding vote to meet the cost of new buildings, and were encouraged to do this by the Government. The sum now stands at £25,000. The school meal system has been restricted or abolished for children in other racial groups. Where possible, voluntary agencies are carrying on with this much-needed service among African children, with the help of such philanthropic provision of balanced foodstuffs as is provided by the Kupugani Organization.

Secondary and Teacher Training

A number of Churches opted to retain the wardenship of the hostels of their post-primary boarding institutions when the Government took over the administration of the teaching. This attempt to continue to provide character training within a residential setting has been fraught with difficulties. Divided loyalties, suspicion of the church hostel-wardens by government principals, the treatment by the latter of every little unrest among pupils as evidence of political activity and the calling in of police to deal with what were only minor discipline cases, all this has made the task of the wardens at times nearly intolerable. There is no question that the morale of these boarding schools and colleges is very low. Some of the best of the old church institutions have disappeared altogether, owing to their having been situated in what are now white areas. While an outside observer may hold that there was often too much rigidity in the old pattern of church institution, he cannot but feel that the gratuitous breaking up of established traditions in corporate school life has been a serious injury to African education.

Adult Education

New regulations introduced in 1957 seriously altered the basis of much African adult education in the towns. Government grants towards the payment of teachers were withdrawn and the cost transferred to fees. Voluntary white teachers, who had sustained many of the classes both at primary and post-primary level, were no longer permitted to work in African areas. Schools held in white areas were discouraged.[1]

---

[1] (a) In Durban there were twenty-five active night schools, providing literacy courses and classes up to St. V. This group had a white director, an all-African staff, and more than 3,500 adult African students. The state grants were withdrawn, and all the classes have closed.

(b) A school with seventy students run by white volunteers for dock-workers in the harbour area of Cape Town was allowed to continue although in a white area. During 1961, the General Manager of Railways gave instructions to close the school; but some nine months later, after repeated representation, the Department of Bantu Education agreed to its revival on condition that it was staffed exclusively by African teachers. It has proved difficult to find suitable African teachers able to travel to the area, and to raise funds to pay them.

University Education

Prior to 1959, when University *apartheid* was introduced, non-white students could attend the open Universities of Cape Town and the Witwatersrand where a practice of 'academic non-segregation' was followed, could enrol at the University of Natal in segregated classes, and could become students at the non-white University College of Fort Hare taking degrees of Rhodes University. They could also study by means of correspondence courses at the University of South Africa, with its headquarters in Pretoria.

Since 1960, no new non-white students have been allowed to enrol as undergraduates at white Universities. The only University education open to Africans is at the University College of Fort Hare and the two new Colleges, built in remote country areas, the University College of the North at Turfloop and the University College of Zululand at Ngoya. These are established on an ethnic basis: Xhosa at Fort Hare; Sotho, Venda and Tsonga at Turfloop; Zulu and Swazi at Ngoya. The degrees taken are those of the University of South Africa. These Colleges are under the administration of the Minister of Bantu Education who has final powers regarding the admission of students.

The buildings of the new Colleges and their equipment are good and their staffs keen. They cannot, however, provide day-by-day contacts between students of different racial groups, or even between those of different language groups among Africans. Nor can they provide opportunities for urban Africans to take part-time courses.

Appendix. The following comment on Bantu Education by Dr Ben Marais, in *The Two Faces of Africa*, should be recorded:

'I have great sympathy with our white group and with the South African Government in this matter of Bantu Education. It constitues a tremendous obligation fraught with every conceivable problem. For three million to educate and raise twelve million is a great burden, but in terms of emerging Africa, of human relations and of Christian service a tremendous opportunity. For these reasons the question must be asked: has the take-over of Bantu Education in 1954 really in all respects yielded what could have been expected, or is popularly claimed? Is the picture as bright as often presented? If and when one faces South Africa's critics or even friends overseas one soon discovers that they view the whole matter in somewhat other than our traditional contexts and ask awkward questions. For this reason and for the sake of all South

---

(c) Eight schools in white suburbs of Pretoria were forced to close. They catered for domestic servants accommodated in the white areas who found it impractical to travel out to the African townships in the evenings to attend classes.

Africans interested in these matters the following comments are made to give a fuller and more balanced total picture.

'The enrolment and figures for teachers, university graduates and expenditure can be very misleading if not elaborated upon. To see the picture as a whole some other facts must be taken into consideration. . . . It is difficult in the light of these figures to refute the accusation of South Africa's critics that in terms of South African total budget what is spent on African development in general and on African education in particular is very low indeed. Critics point out that according to the 1962 Budget figures only 4 per cent of the budget was spent on African development, i.e. the development of 69 per cent of our total population. The total Bantu Education vote was only about half of the police vote and the percentage from general revenue towards the schooling of the African 69 per cent of the population was barely two-sevenths of 1 per cent of the national income of South Africa. Viewed from this angle the claim that South Africa does more than any other African country takes on a different complexion. The question is how much does South Africa, Ghana, or Nigeria respectively spend in terms of their total budgets or resources? Naturally, a very rich country can do more than a poor country in terms of actual expenditure. It must also be pointed out that the per capita expenditure on African pupils has been steadily decreasing in recent years. Whereas the cost per African pupil amounted to R17·08 in 1953-54, that amount had dropped to R12·46 in 1960-61. The Minister of Bantu Education attributes the decrease to better control and to the faster expansion of primary than of secondary education. "Better control" included savings on books, school feeding, equipment, etc., and enabled the diversion of considerable funds to the maintenance of the tribal university colleges. . . .

'The figures for per capita expenditure of the different races speak for themselves and need no elaboration except to stress the fact that in Bantu Education today only 3·2 per cent of the total enrolment is in secondary education (2·5 in 1948 but 3·5 in 1953 under Provincial control). Bantu Education mainly concerns children in the lower standards, the bulk between Sub-Standard A and St. II. This is almost dramatically illustrated by the 1950 enrolment figures. Of the 200,000 African pupils enrolled in 1950, 894 sat for the Matriculation examination in 1962. Of these 532 failed and only 4 gained first-class passes. This was Bantu Education's best result for years. We know, also, that the 3,800 Bantu students in Teacher Training Colleges must be compared with the 6,000 in 1954 when the service was much smaller. On the face of the Minister's own figures it means that between 1948 and 1962 there was only one new teacher for every eighty new pupils enrolled. Before 1954 African education was a charge on general revenue. After the Act of 1954, the charge on general revenue for African schools was frozen at

R13 million and all future expansion has to be borne entirely by the African people themselves. Though there are perfectly good reasons for much of the difference in unit costs between white and African pupils the gap has increasingly widened instead of narrowed. This is alarming. At least one authority claims that whereas in 1954 eight times as much was spent on a white pupil as on an African pupil, the gap has widened to 14 to 1 in 1963!'

VII · RESIDENCE PERMITS IN TOWNS

The *Bantu Affairs Act of* 1963-64 confirms the trend of earlier legislation and in particular the *Urban Areas Act of* 1945, in providing that the sole test of the right of an African to remain in an urban area is that his labour is required there. The following examples have all been possible since 1945 under the Urban Areas Act of that year.

1. An African who was born in a town and lived there continuously for fifty years, but then left to reside elsewhere for any period, even two weeks, is not entitled as of right to return to the town where he was born and to remain there for more than seventy-two hours. If he does, he is guilty of a criminal offence punishable by a fine not exceeding ten pounds, or, in default, imprisonment for a period not exceeding two months, unless he has obtained a permit to do so.

2. An African who, although not born there, has lived continuously in a town for fifty years and is still living there, loses his right to remain there for more than seventy-two hours if he commits a criminal offence for which he is sentenced to a fine exceeding fifty pounds.

3. An African who has lived continuously in a town for twenty years and is still living there has no right to remain there for more than seventy -two hours once he has accepted employment outside that town.

4. An African who has lived continuously in a town for fourteen years and still lives and works there is not entitled as of right to remain there for more than seventy-two hours.

5. An African who has lived continuously in a town for nine years, is still living there and has worked continuously throughout that period for one employer, is not entitled as of right to remain there for more than seventy-two hours.

6. An African who has since birth resided continuously in a town is not entitled as of right to have living with him in that town for more than seventy-two hours a married daughter, a son who has reached the age of eighteen, a niece, a nephew or a grandchild.

7. If an African born in a town has lived there continuously for fifty years, no friend of his who is an African is entitled as of right to visit and remain with him for more than seventy-two hours.

H

8. If an African was born in a town, has lived there continuously for fourteen years and has during that period worked continuously for one employer for nine years, neither his wife, his unmarried daughter nor his son aged eighteen (although each is completely dependent upon him) is entitled as of right to live with him for more than seventy-two hours.

The following is a summary of the new provisions enacted this year:

1. Delegated power to forbid any African entry into any area outside the Reserves, or to seek or take employment except through State labour bureaux;

2. The establishment of 'aid centres' to accommodate Africans refused employment in urban areas, until they have accepted work offered to them or until they have been 'endorsed out';

3. The extension of labour regulations, including influx control, to all parts of the country, excepting the Reserves;

4. The abolition of the existing right of urban-born Africans, and those in continuous employment for fifteen years, to remain in the urban areas. In terms of the Bill, labour bureaux will be set up in every 'prescribed area', including farming areas, through which all African labour will be channelled. It is now an offence for any employer to employ an African without the permission of a labour bureau.

VIII · CONDITIONS IN THE AFRICAN TOWNSHIPS

Address delivered by the Rev. J. C. Mvusi, of the Methodist Church, New Brighton Township, Port Elizabeth, on 'Meeting men in the cities—the problems of urbanization in African townships', at the National Conference of the Christian Council of South Africa, on 'The New Dimensions of Mission for South Africa Today', Johannesburg, 21st-22nd May 1964.

Rapid industrialization in South Africa since World War II is responsible for large concentrations of African communities now living on the fringes of all the large cities. Two things have contributed towards the creation of this position: (1) poverty in the Reserves; (2) the ever-increasing labour demands of expanding industries in urban areas.

The stream of able-bodied African men has flown from the rural to the urban centres in increasing strength during the last quarter-century. Both urbanization and industrialization are responsible to a large extent for the rapid social and economic changes which obtain in African townships today. The first of these changes is from a traditional communal system of living to the individualistic western way of life, and the resultant adjustment from a cattle to a money economy. But the main problems of urbanization in African townships arise chiefly from the country's economic system which is based on migrant labour. The migratory labour system may not be peculiar to South Africa but it is here where it affects radically the life of one section of a multi-racial society. To the African men and their families, migrant labour entails sacrifice of human life for the profits of the industrialist. Legislation such as the Bantu Laws Amendment Act bears testimony to the view that the African is an alien and sojourner in the urban areas of his motherland. Stringent regulations now compel African men to live for 353 days of the year away from their wives. Visits to husbands are by permit and for limited periods. Children are prevented from enjoying town facilities for higher education.

Social evils which are sapping the very life-blood and character of the people in these townships are associated in the first instance with the problem of housing. Single quarters for thousands of men (married and unmarried) are provided in barracks or compounds. In most cases these are healthy. Men are given good and nourishing food and sporting facilities are available, and yet these are the very cells that first introduced African men to the town evil of homosexuality. These men fall an easy prey to the big finance dagga runner and the shebeen queen, because they are removed far from the social unit, the home. On the other hand, married quarters are located in the same proximity. This arrangement has added its quota to the alarmingly high rate of births out of wedlock.[1] Unwanted children are born daily, thus adding fat to the raging fire of juvenile delinquency. The houses are the sub-economic type suited to the needs of the low-income group of unskilled labourers, but inadequate for the average African family which is not just father, mother and child but a handful of relatives also. Privacy therefore is not possible. Men have little or no choice of house and locality. For the men who can afford a better type of house, private ownership is fast running out. Money which would otherwise provide for comfortable homes is spent in buying motor-cars. One peculiarity which has no parallel elsewhere is that by some sort of agreement between a married man (with a family in the country) and a single woman known as *Masihla-lisane*, meaning 'let us live together as man and wife', a family is raised in town, with the result that one in the homelands suffers from neglect and starvation.

The modern rapidly changing conditions of today are not only confusing the African but will not admit the use of his former tribal sanctions which assisted in stabilizing public life. There is very slow progress towards mutual responsibility and public conscience in the townships. For instance, how much concern is there for one's neighbour

[1] The figure in the New Brighton township is approximately 60 per cent.

as in days gone by? Here is the sort of thing you will find: Roland, the youngest son of the Rev. G. B. Molefe of New Brighton, Port Elizabeth, was done to death by a *tsotsi* for protecting a young girl in the street who was being molested. No one came to his aid because no one dared to come out for fear of being stabbed. Fear is paralysing evening worship. Daylight attacks are made on well-behaved school-going young people just because they refuse to toe the line with the underworld. The position has been aggravated more by fear, secrecy and suspicion which have gripped the people from the time of the banning of organizations like the African National Congress. The very atmosphere is choking the spiritual life of the people. The growing number of people who are doubting Christianity as a way of life for Africans is casting yet another shadow. The sects thrive on ancestor-worship as a way out because Christianity is the white man's religion. The Church is not interested in the national aspirations of the people. The young generation now growing up in these townships fear no kind of authority, neither gaol nor death and the worst of all, not even God.

The problems I have referred to in this brief and sketchy outline call for a new approach on the part of the Christian Churches. Unless they are prepared to plan and consult with a view to action together in a new programme in which all hands must play some part regardless of colour, creed or caste, they are doomed to fail. In order to win this country for Christ, the first big impact by the Christian forces must revolutionize afresh all our large concentrations in the cities.

IX · SECTION 17 OF THE
GENERAL LAW AMENDMENT ACT[1]*

The Meeting on 24th May 1964

1. On 24th May 1964, the Secretary of the Working Party attended a remarkable service in the City Hall, Cape Town. Thousands packed the Hall, with relay to a large overflow meeting. As it was the Cape Pro-

* (To be suspended as from Jan. 1965. It could be reimposed by proclamation.)

[1] Section 17 of Act No. 37 (1963) reads as follows:

17. (1) Notwithstanding anything to the contrary in any law contained, any commissioned officer as defined in section one of the Police Act 1958 (Act No. 7 of 1958) may from time to time without warrant arrest or cause to be arrested any person whom he suspects upon reasonable grounds of having committed or intending or having intended to commit any offence under the Suppression of Communism Act 1950 (Act No. 44 of 1950), or under the last-mentioned Act as applied by the Unlawful Organizations Act 1960 (Act No. 34 of 1960), or the offence of sabotage, or who in his opinion is in possession of any information relating to the commission of any such offence, or the intention to commit any such offence, and detain such person, or cause him to be detained, in custody for interrogation in connection with the commission of, or intention to commit, such offence,

vince,[1] black, Coloured and white faces appeared side by side in the audience; South African citizens of all races were united to their purpose: a resolve to present a solemn petition to the Government not to renew the 90-day Clause.

2. The remarkable character of the meeting derived from the fact that it was the first time in the history of South Africa that leaders of the Christian, Jewish and Moslem faiths had all joined in a single declaration to the President of the Republic. Likewise for the first time, many former judges and a former Chief Justice were present at the meeting to mark the protest of the judiciary. Adopted unanimously, after a moving service of intercession, the Declaration read as follows:

> Inasmuch as we believe it is a fundamental tenet of justice that there should be no imprisonment without trial and that access to the normal protections of the rule of law should be accorded to everyone and that Section 17 of the General Law Amendment Act (commonly known as the '90-day detention clause') is a tragic breach and negation of this principle, and a violation of the moral law, and an offence to religious conscience, we declare our strongest condemnation of this clause on moral grounds, and appeal to those in authority not to re-promulgate it when it comes under review.

3. On 30th June 1964 the Minister of Justice re-promulgated the Section.

The Effects of Section 17

4. What in fact does the Section do? It empowers a police officer to arrest without warrant any person suspected for any reason whatsoever

---

at any place he may think fit, until such person has, in the opinion of the Commissioner of the South African Police, replied satisfactorily to all questions at the said interrogation, but no such person shall be so detained for more than 90 days on any particular occasion when he is so arrested.

(2) No person shall, except with the consent of the Minister of Justice or a commissioned officer as aforesaid, have access to any person detained under sub-section (1): provided that not less than once during each week such person shall be visited in private by the magistrate, or an additional or assistant magistrate, of the district in which he is detained.

(3) No court shall have jurisdiction to order the release from custody of any person so detained, but the said Minister may at any time direct that any such person be released from custody.

(4) (a) Subject to the provisions of paragraphs (b) and (c), sub-sections (1) to (3) inclusive shall be in operation until the 30th day of June 1964, and for such periods thereafter not exceeding twelve months at a time as the State President may from time to time by proclamation in the *Gazette* determine.

(b) Any proclamation under paragraph (a) may be issued at any time, whether or not the said sub-sections have then ceased to be in operation.

(c) The State President may at any time by like proclamation suspend the operation of the said sub-sections or withdraw any proclamation issued under paragraph (a).

[1]At the Johannesburg meeting the week before, only whites were allowed to attend, as it was also held in the City Hall—a public building.

of being in possession of information concerning certain political crimes, even if that person is known to be innocent of any crime, and detain him without trial for any number of 90-day periods in any size cell, under any conditions he thinks suitable, deprived of all human contact except that of a gaoler and a once-a-week visiting magistrate, isolated from family and Church, with no right to legal or medical aid or right of access to reading matter or writing material, with only two half-hours of exercise each day—perhaps—and liable to interrogation at any time, and for any length of time, until an answer that satisfies the police is given.

The Two Major Objections to Sections 17

5. The first principle the Section contravenes is the rule of law. A former Chief Justice, the Hon. Mr Justice Centlivres, has stated:

> Section 17 need never have been introduced. The law was already powerful enough, before Section 17 was passed by Parliament, to deal with any case of sabotage or terrorism without degrading justice and spurning the rule of law.

In this view he was supported by the following former judges, who all identified themselves with the religious communities' appeal given in paragraph 2 above—the Hon. Sir John Murray, the Hon. Richard Feetham, the Hon. Leopold Greenberg, the Hon. Leslie Blackwell, the Hon. Israel Maisels. Yet more telling support would have come (one may suppose) from the late Dr D. F. Malan, later Prime Minister. At a time of alleged subversive activities and sabotage during World War II, he stated:

> Whether a Union subject is guilty or not guilty makes no difference, but it is his human right, of which we cannot deprive him, to be tried before an impartial court of justice.

6. The second principle the Section 17 violates is that of humane treatment of prisoners. Under the Geneva Convention no prisoner of war may be subjected to any single punishment of solitary confinement exceeding thirty days. Normal South African prison regulations prohibit more than two days' solitary confinement in one week. The reason for this are medical and psychological. Sixty South African medical specialists appealed to the Minister in the following terms:

'As the time approaches for reappraisal of the "90-day" detention clause, we, as medical specialists, psychiatrists and psychologists, consider it our duty to draw the attention of the Government and the public to the possible serious consequences of this form of detention on the mental condition of the detainees.

'The psychiatric study of political prisoners subjected to periods of solitary confinement in various countries indicates that this experience is associated with intense distress and impairment of certain mental functions. Numerous experimental studies support this evidence.

'We submit that the exposure of individuals to acute suffering and mental impairment for indefinite periods of time is not less abhorrent than physical torture. No cause can justify the injury, whether physical or mental, of persons who have not been found guilty of an offence by the courts of the country.

'We also wish to draw attention to the existence of scientific evidence which suggests that prolonged isolation may cause a disturbance of judgment to the point where the individual's testimony is no longer reliable . . . the results of interrogation of detainees in this state may well be untrustworthy.

'We feel, therefore, that the present system of detention in solitary confinement is inhuman and unjustifiable, and we appeal for its abolition.'

7. The Head of the Department of Psychology of the University of Cape Town, Professor Danziger, emphasized:

'It has been found that mental deterioration takes place during prolonged solitary confinement. This deterioration might not be obvious either to the prisoner or gaoler.

'There is the serious possibility that a man's mental function may become impaired to the point where ability to distinguish between reality and fiction begins to become defective.

'During solitary confinement it is found that the prisoner becomes more malleable mentally and receptive to suggestion.

'If he is given an opportunity to talk he may say anything which seems to be appropriate, or to be desired by his interrogator, for in his impaired and befuddled state he may be unable to tell what is "actually true" from what "might be" or "should be" true.

'It also supposes that individual subjects become unable to distinguish which of these thoughts and images correspond to reality and which do not. Delusions and hallucinations may develop.

'The use of solitary confinement as a method of obtaining reliable information is extremely dangerous.

'Solitary confinement may have, to some people, the same effect as physical torture. People who have been subjected to both solitary confinement and physical torture have indicated that the former is infinitely worse to endure.'

8. Small wonder that the Minister of Justice said to Parliament:

'Anyone who tries to deny that this clause could lead to misuse is

a fool. I am painfully aware of this fact. It is not a very nice thing to
see a human being broken. I have seen it.[1]

The Four Broken Undertakings of the Government

9. When the Section was debated, the Minister of Justice promised
four things to Parliament. None of these promises has been kept.

(1) Mr Vorster gave a solemn undertaking, on more than one
occasion in Parliament, that 'in no case' would detention last
'for longer than 90 days'. He stressed this promise by adding:
'Note well, I am limiting the period to 90 days . . . this Government has shown that it is a Government which can be trusted
with powers of this kind.' (Hansard 24/4/63, col. 4657, 4874,
4926 and Senate Hansard 29/4/63, col. 2702.)

   In practice, many people have been detained for successive
periods of 90 days. One man was detained three times in
succession under the '90-day' clause, and when brought to trial
was discharged. Two mothers were detained for two periods of
90 days. Teenagers have had the same experience. Thirteen
persons, after 90-day treatment, were brought to trial and discharged—but re-arrested as they left the court. One man was
detained in solitary confinement from 10th May to 4th November 1963. He was allowed one visitor, once, during these 180
days' detention.

(2) Mr Vorster assured Parliament that 'in every case the next of
kin are always advised'.

   In practice, this is by no means always so. Detainees have
been moved about from prison to prison, from town to country
gaol, from Cape Town to Pretoria and back, and the next of kin
can very seldom keep track of where they are. Mr Ngudle died
in gaol and was buried before his wife was advised. One 16-
year-old boy was detained on 11th June 1963; only on 17th
October did his mother discover where he was.

(3) Mr Vorster guaranteed that he would not keep the '90-day'
detention law on the Statute Book 'a moment longer than it is necessary. . . . It is not part of our permanent law' (Hansard 24/4/63,
col. 4845). And again, 'I appreciate it is not a provision that is
proper in peace time' (Hansard 24/4/63, col. 4657). Later he
stated: 'We will keep the "90-day" clause to meet more of a
potential than an existing emergency.'

(4) Mr Vorster stated: 'The Act is not to isolate or to punish them
(detainees); it is not to prevent them from conspiring with other
people; it is *to obtain information from them;* that is the official
and only reason.'

[1] Hansard of 24th April 1963, col. 4853.

In practice, the police use this clause admittedly for penal purposes. A police officer, Lt Swanepoel, has described it as 'a mighty weapon' in police hands. Det. Sgt Card said (29th January 1964); 'I did not use the 90 days for questioning them: I merely used it to keep them in custody to prevent interference from outside.'[1] One woman spent her full 90 days of detention without any interrogation.

The Allegations of Police Torture

10. The evidence is so strong, and such public knowledge in South Africa, that this unpleasant fact cannot be passed over in any summary of the implementation of Section 17.

11. The court records show that many ex-detainee state witnesses have admitted maltreatment and torture. One of them swore on oath that he was not only beaten up, but subjected to electric shock treatment. In the Ngudle inquest, six witnesses were prepared to give evidence of being 'beaten up'. A state witness in the case of State *v.* Matshaba (T.P.D. 29/11/63) said: 'He (the policeman) hit me. . . he struck me with his fist in my face . . . he kicked me in the ribs. He threatened me with starvation. The third time I agreed to what he wanted me to write down.' At Goodwood, in Cape Town, in the case of State *v.* Potje, a state witness admitted torture by electric shocks.

Full parliamentary discussions of documented allegations, taken from court records, of physical torture, including electric shock treatments, of 90-day detainees by the police appear in Hansard on 23rd January and 6th February 1964. Subsequent denials by the Government that the case was typical do not erase the court record of the Bloemfontein case in March 1964. A police officer said, under oath, in this case (13/3/64): 'I don't think there is a police station in the country that doesn't use violence during questioning.' The use of a suffocating plastic bag was 'common in investigations'. He said he had been taught in the Bloemfontein police station to suffocate natives, to make them helpless by trussing them with handcuffs and a stick, and to use the electric shock machine. He said he knew it was illegal, but he always 'tried not to leave marks'. Evidence was given that when the shock machine could not be found in its usual place in the prison garage, a pupil constable was sent to get a police officer's private machine from his home.

12. In 1962, according to statements made by the Minister of Justice, there were 17 cases of policemen assaulting witnesses in criminal trials, and 44 assaults by the police on prisoners. On 30th April 1963, Senator Rall (United Party) stated that when he was a magistrate,

---

[1] This use of the Act is illegal, since detention is authorized only 'for interrogation'. But, since sub-section (3) excludes the jurisdiction of the Courts to restrain, change or correct illegality, the Section sanctions abuse of these powers.

Many a day when I was on the Bench I saw a bloody face in the box and would accuse the police of having manhandled the prisoner. . . . In one case, because of my objections, a certain policeman who was always bullying accused prisoners was transferred to the north coast of Natal. Two years later, he was sentenced to six and a half years of imprisonment in the Supreme Court for having brutally murdered a prisoner.

Conclusion

13. No comment is needed on the following summary of the effects of Section 17, *of what is known publicly*, during the period 11th March 1963–11th March 1964.

Total detained under Section 17 of the General Law Amendment Act 1963	682*
Number detained for more than 90 days	61
Number detained for more than 180 days	8
(Note: 3 women served more than one 90-day period.)	
Number released without charge (as at 21st Jan. 1964)	233
Number of teenagers (16-19 years)	39
Number who died by hanging	2
Number examined by psychiatrists or sent to mental institutions	5
Number still detained (as at 7th April 1964)	73
Number of detainees who escaped	5
Number who gave evidence for State under promise of indemnity	46
Number who received indemnity	36
Number who were pregnant at time of detention (one held from 25th June–15th Nov.; one from 2nd Aug.–5th Sept.)	2
Number complaining of assaults by policemen or warders	49
(26 alleged hitting and kicking; 19 alleged they were kicked, hit and electrically shocked, with sacks over heads; 1 electrically shocked; 3 assaults.)	
*Number detained between 25/2/64 and 7/4/64	41
Number released without charge	22

14. Instead of comment, one may recall the words of an Afrikaner poet:

> As jy'n trotse volk verkneg
> Word opstand teen die reg sy reg.

> If you enslave a proud people,
> Resistance to the law becomes its right.

—and find the echo of this draconian legislation in the statement made by Nelson Mandela in his own defence.[1]

[1] Cp. para. 76 of the Study Report.

X · SUMMARY OF APARTHEID LEGISLATION
SINCE 1950

1. *The Population Registration Act of 1950 and 1952.* The law defined and classified into racial categories—'whites', 'coloured', 'Natives', and other subdivisions to cover Asians, etc.
2. *Separate Representation of Voters Act, 1951 and 1956.* This provided that the Coloured voters in the Cape should be removed from the common roll and placed on a separate roll to elect four white representatives.
3. *The Group Areas of Act 1950 and 1957, with subsequent amendments.* This law extended the powers of the authorities to bring about complete territorial and residential separation according to race over the whole country.
4. *The Bantu Authorities Act, 1951 and 1959.* This provided for the creation of tribal authorities in certain areas, and for the legal consideration of Africans living in urban areas as aliens in South Africa. The 1959 Act abolished the Parliamentary representation of Africans and provided for the appointment of, initially, five Commissioners-General to represent the Government. The Transkei Constitution Act of 1963 provided for the election of a Transkeian Assembly with limited powers and under the jurisdiction of the South African Government.
5. *The Native Laws Amendment Acts of 1952, 1956 and 1957.* These laws introduce controls over the so-called 'influx' of Africans into urban or non-African areas as classified by the Group Areas Authority. Under this law any African born in South Africa can visit an urban area for up to seventy-two hours without obtaining a special permit. Stringent conditions for the permanent residence of Africans in urban or 'white' areas are provided for, and the local authorities are given powers to order an African to leave any area if 'it is considered that his presence is detrimental to the maintenance of peace and order'. Under this provision many political workers and trade unionists have been banished to distant regions.
6. *Reservation of Separate Amenities Act, 1953.* This legalized and enforced racial segregation practised in public transport, schools, places of entertainment, church, hospitals, clubs and 'similar institutions'.
7. *Native Labour Act of 1953 and the Industrial Conciliation Act of 1956.* These laws redefined the term 'employee' to exclude Africans; prevented the registration of trade unions having African members; and prohibited strikes by African workers. Mixed trade unions (i.e. containing both white and non-white workers) could no longer be 'registered'. Provision was made for 'job reservation', that is, for

specified types of work to be reserved for persons of specified racial groups.

8. *The Bantu Education Act*, 1959. The control of African education was transferred to the Ministry of Native Affairs. No schools were to be established without the Minister's permission, and he was given wide powers to make regulations covering levels and standards of African education. The Act prohibited the entry of non-whites to the existing 'mixed' universities, and separate racial universities were created. It was this Act that occasioned the famous protest of all the staff and students of Witwatersrand University, who marched through the streets of Johannesburg proclaiming the inviolability of academic freedom in a democratic society. A plaque commemorates this at the entry to the aula, so that the remaining (white) students see it each day on entering the main university building.

XI · STATEMENT BY THE CENTRAL COMMITTEE OF THE WORLD COUNCIL OF CHURCHES ON RACIAL AND ETHNIC TENSION

August, 1963

'When we are given Christian insight the whole pattern of racial discrimination is seen as an unutterable offence against God, to be endured no longer, so that the very stones cry out. In such moments we understand more fully the meaning of the Gospel, and the duty of both Church and Christian.'

In these words the Second Assembly of the World Council of Churches, at its meeting in 1954 in the United States, declared its conviction at a time when the struggle against discrimination arising from racial and ethnic differences was world-wide. Today, as we meet, the struggle is approaching its climax. Whole peoples are determined to endure no longer the patterns of segregation which deny them dignity, and which deny dignity to man himself so long as they remain anywhere in the world.

The struggle gains in intensity, in the United States where we now meet, in South Africa, and in other continents and countries. Men, women and children, Christian and non-Christian alike, are laying aside thought for personal safety, are imprisoned, are risking life itself, are incurring the deep suffering of loneliness, are enduring the dislocation of family life, are demonstrating a supreme courage amid natural fears, and are refraining from the retaliation which uses the brutal means of their oppressors. To all these, we give whole-hearted support, praying that they may be strengthened, and that their goal may soon be achieved. We give thanks to God that he has called many Christians to share in the leadership of this struggle for racial equality. We ask all Christians and the Churches as such to join them and to support them.

We acknowledge with deep shame that many Christians through hesitation and inaction are not engaged in this struggle, or are on the wrong side of it. We therefore repeat, with all the conviction at our command, what the Assembly said in 1954, that 'any form of segregation based on race, colour or ethnic origin is contrary to the Gospel, and is incompatible with the Christian doctrine of man and with the nature of the Church of Christ'. Wherever and whenever any of us Christians deny this, by action or inaction, we betray Christ and the fellowship which bears His name.

We plead with every Church in every place to search its inner attitude and its practice, to insure that its fellowship includes all who believe, without discrimination and in full love, and to take every step to strengthen all whose witness is weak to speak and act with courage. The first requirement for the Churches in respect of race is that they themselves remove racial barriers in their own fellowship. Only thus can their claim to work for justice, human dignity and brotherhood be made credible. Only thus can they pray for and minister to oppressed and oppressors alike, as the love of Christ constrains them to do. Only so, in these days, can they faithfully preach the Gospel.

The grave racial conflict in the Republic of South Africa cries out for solution. Opportunities for mutal communication between the racial communities in the Republic have been severely restricted. All these communities are the tragic victims of increasing insecurity and fear. In the last years the Government has enacted legislation of the most repressive character which takes away the very foundations of personal freedom and security, and affects the whole atmosphere of personal and social life. Millions of Africans are condemned to live in areas of 'separate development' under government schemes conceived in such restrictive terms that those to whom they apply can neither trust nor accept them.

This extreme crisis summons all Christian people to recognize and accept their common responsibility. At the Cottesloe Consultation of 1960, church leaders of South Africa showed a way of reversing the trend towards increasing conflict. The white Christians in the Republic must reconsider the way the Churches have gone since then. They are urged to a determination to repudiate—by deeds as well as words—all that weakens their witness to Christ, in whom all men are one. We call on Christians to remember in their prayers those of all races in South Africa who take great risks and incur severe penalties in the cause of justice and human solidarity. Christians outside the Republic must work to inform world opinion and to impress upon other countries and governments their responsibility in respect of this great crisis. The pursuit by governments of selfish national interests, particularly in the economic sphere, in their relations with South Africa can do much to defer the realization of racial justice for all her peoples. All Christians must do everything in their power to show their care for the victims of discrimination, and to relieve the needs of refugees from the Republic.

Although most Africans have abandoned hope of an internal solution to a situation which appears to be beyond it, all Christians must pray and work for a just and peaceful solution. They must urge the Government of the Republic to re-establish contact with the African, Coloured and Indian communities; to lose no time in reversing the political trend; in securing full political, civil and economic rights for all members of these communities, particularly for those in urban areas, and to restore justice to all.

Free communication and contact between the various racial groups and their leaders and between them and other leaders of the nation in every sphere of life is essential. Isolation will lead to conflict; communication is the prerequisite of peace. We ask that Christians especially take the lead in crossing the barriers which now keep men from even speaking to one another.

We cannot but remind the white population of South Africa, and especially the Christians within it, that to continue the present policy of race relations will inevitably mean increased isolation from the rest of the world. That policy is one with which peoples throughout the world are in profound disagreement. Moreover, it has established within South Africa a spirit of entrenchment rather than of openness. Both factors work toward the isolation of South Africa. We appeal to white Christians so to labour with their fellow citizens and their Government, that rigidity and isolation may give way to openness and collaboration.

The movement to secure full human and civil rights for negro citizens in the United States has now become a tide which cannot be turned back. Nor is it any longer a purely internal issue. It is rather an integral part of world-wide racial tension, and as such has become a matter of deep concern for Christians everywhere. The Central Committee pays tribute to all those in the United States, negro, white and others, who have suffered in this cause. It commends those parishes, individuals and Christian organizations who are struggling to remove this blemish from the life of the nation. It laments that there are still white citizens desperately trying to perpetuate patterns of racial segregation in Church and school, in housing and employment, and in public accommodation. In the centennial year of the Emancipation Proclamation and in the week of the unprecedented demonstration in Washington for civil rights, the Central Committee calls on the Churches of the United States to intensify efforts to eliminate all forms of racial discrimination from every aspect of life in their country. The Churches have much to do in order to bring their practice in race relations into accord with their policy. The time has come for them to work to get the international implications and ramifications of the crisis understood. The time has come for them to strive together to help remove every trace of discrimination from the national life. The time has come for them to redouble efforts to develop genuine communication between negro and other citizens to fulfil the ministry of reconciliation.

The demand for racial and ethnic equality is being made in many places, and will continue until it is attained everywhere in full. We remind ourselves that the references to South Africa and the United States present a challenge to all our consciences, to do in our own countries, cities and Churches all that we should for racial justice and Christian fellowship. The solution demanded requires radical change in long-established patterns of thought and action. Wherever fear of such change may exist, we must recall that when God is present, as surely He is in this matter, there is no need for fear. One further grave consequence of the struggle for racial equality is that it sets up barriers to open communication between individuals, between races, between governments, between organizations, and even between Churches. But openness and free communication are indispensable to the attainment of the goal.

The promise of the Holy Spirit is the guarantee that these things are possible.

XII · THE STRENGTH OF SOUTH AFRICA'S ARMED FORCES IN RELATION TO THOSE OF THE ADDIS ABABA POWERS

Land Forces

1. The Republic of South Africa has a full-time army of about 15,000, and she claims to be able to put 250,000 into the field at short notice.

2. The Southern Rhodesian army numbers 3,400. Portugal is reported to have some 9,000 troops in Angola and 5,000 in Mozambique.

3. Armies which might contribute contingents to the 'African Liberation Army' are the following:

Algeria	70,000
Egypt	100,000
Morocco	35,000

Tunisia	20,000
Ethiopia	29,000
Ghana	8,000
Nigeria	7,000
Kenya	3,000
Somalia	6,000
Northern Rhodesia	2,000
Libya	3,000
Guinea	5,000
Cameroons	2,700
Congo (Leopoldville)	29,000

4. These figures take no account of para-military police, and do not reflect differences in equipment and quality of training. In any case, they reflect little, for the ability to mount an expeditionary force is not a function of the size of an army, but rather of its internal commitments, its administrative backing and its logistics support. In 1960 some 8,000 African troops were sent to the Congo, but they were largely dependent on American air transport for getting there.

Air Forces

5. Various countries have training and communications aircraft, but the military value of such 'planes is largely confined to internal security. The key elements in the military aerial balance of power are long-range reconnaisance and fighter-cum-strike aircraft. Very old fighters are piston-engined; more recent ones are jets. The most important index of the quality of a jet fighter is its speed. They may be classified on this basis into the subsonic ones, those that fly just above the speed of sound, which is Mach 1·0, and those which are capable of Mach 2·0 or above.

6. The Republic of South Africa possesses 16 Mirage III Mach 2·0 strike aircraft, supplied by France in 1963. In December, 1964 Britain will begin supplying the first of 16 Buccaneer Mk II naval strike aircraft, which fly at Mach 1·2, and would be able to attack blockading British or American aircraft carriers which formed part of a United Nations' Sanctions Task Force. The subsonic jet fighters include 38 American Sabres and the 30 British-built Vampires of the auxiliary Citizen Air Force. Eight Shackleton long-range maritime reconnaissance bombers are operational, and 6 Canberra subsonic light jet bombers and high-altitude reconnaissance 'planes have also been supplied by Britain in 1963-64. The Canberras are at present assigned to training duties.

7. The Egyptian air force comprises 300-350 warplanes operational, including 50 MIG-21s, 100 MIG-19s, 80 MIG-17s, 25 TU-16s and 75 IL-28s. The MIG series are all jet fighters; the latter two super-

sonic, and the MIG-21s are capable of Mach 2.0. The Algerians already have 10 MIG-15s, and more are reported to be under order from the Soviet Union. The Moroccan air force includes 12 MIG-17s and 2 IL-28s. Tupolev 16s and Ilyushin 28s are medium and light bombers respectively.

8. Apart from the Imperial Ethiopian Air Force, which has 15 Sabres and 20 Swedish Saab-16 fighter bombers, which are now obsolescent, and the Somalis, who have some MIG-15 trainers plus a few old piston-engined F-51 Mustangs of last war vintage, the only other state in Africa with any warplanes is Southern Rhodesia. She has 12 Canberras, 12 Hunter and 15 Vampire subsonic jet fighters.

9. From this it follows that if the independent African states did not wish to rely on, or were not able to obtain, the full backing of the United Arab Republic, they would have to invest heavily in military aircraft before they would be in a position in which they could challenge the Republic of South Africa.

Naval Forces

10. Egypt easily heads the continent in this respect, with 10,000 men who man 4 destroyers, 6 frigates and corvettes and 8 submarines. The Republic of South Africa comes second, with 3,500 men who maintain 2 destroyers and 6 frigates, the latter including 3 of the latest Whitby class recently supplied by the United Kingdom. Ethiopia keeps 700 men in her light coastal forces. Nigeria and Ghana have 850 and 500 respectively; the former has one frigate on order, and the latter 3 escort vessels. No other states have any significant naval vessels.

Conclusion

11. Overland infiltration into the Republic would be difficult because of the savanna and semi-desert nature of the terrain. Command of the air would, on the other hand, give African states the chance to parachute supplies in to help insurgents. Egyptian submarines could land supplies for guerrilla fighters on the long coastline. The Republic, however, has now built up an air force of such dimensions that the independent African states could only secure this by invoking Egyptian assistance or making very great efforts to build up a modern air force of their own, with planes supplied by the Soviet Union or China. A point relevant to the deployment of air power is the recent statement by Mr L. J. Le Roux, Vice-President of the National Council of Scientific and Industrial Research, that South African scientists are now working on tabun, soman and sarin. These are poisonous gases first developed by the Nazis, and their effectiveness is terrifying. South Africa also has the technical knowledge and industrial capacity to develop atomic weapons

I

if she so decided, and unconfirmed reports indicate that these are under development. The Working Party believes these reports should be treated with caution.

XIII · THE STRATEGIC IMPORTANCE OF THE SIMONSTOWN AGREEMENT

A. *The Simonstown Agreement*

1. The Simonstown Agreement was concluded in 1955,[1] and has been an important factor in British policy towards South Africa. Up to that date, there had been a Royal Navy base at Simonstown, near Cape Town. Thereafter, Britain gave up control of the base, but retained the right to benefit from its facilities, which include a radio transmitter and storage for 3,000 tons of ammunition reserves. The Agreement also provided that the two countries should co-operate in peacetime naval planning for the protection of the Cape sea routes. South Africa placed orders for twenty British-built warships, costing £18,000,000. These warships consisted of 'anti-submarine frigates, coastal mine-sweepers and seaward defence boats'.[2] These warships have now all been supplied, the last of them being the Whitby class anti-submarine frigates, two of which were delivered in 1963, the last as recently as September.[3]

2. In September 1963 Mr Eric Louw, South African Foreign Minister, stated that South Africa might have to terminate the Simonstown Agreement because of Britain's 'unfriendliness'. He later qualified the threat, saying it would apply 'only if Britain imposed sanctions against the Republic'.

3. As a result, the value of the Simonstown Agreement was examined in Whitehall towards the end of last year, not only because of the South African threat to terminate the Agreement in certain circumstances, but also because of the changing characteristics of Britain's strategic requirements, in the light of the development of weapons since the Agreement was concluded in 1955.

4. It is now accepted unofficially that Simonstown is strategically expendable.

5. Nevertheless, the Conservative administration maintained its position. In reply to a question from the Leader of the Opposition, who had asked whether during the period the Prime Minister had been

---

[1] For text, see Cmd. 9520.
[2] Written answer given by the Minister of Defence to Mr F. M. Bennett, M.P., on 29th May 1963—Official Report, col. 130.
[3] That delivered in March is called the *President Kruger*.

in office arms of any kind had been shipped to South Africa outside the list specified in the schedule to the Simonstown Agreement, the Foreign Secretary replied during the last Foreign Affairs debate on 17th June 1964:

> If the Simonstown Agreement is regarded as important—and my hon. friends and I regard it as important—and if our view is that the strategic needs for it remain strong, we must obviously continue to be prepared to provide arms which are necessary for the support of Simonstown and for the self-defence of the country. It is unreasonable to think we can have a total embargo of arms to South Africa, and still expect them to continue with the Simonstown Agreement. That would be quite impossible.[1]

6. The first point in this context is that there are several alternative bases in the Indian and South Atlantic Oceans. The bases in the Indian Ocean are examined in section B below. In the South Atlantic there is St Helena and the Falkland Islands off the tip of South America. Both these have anchorages equal to that of Simonstown, suitable for dockyard repairs. St Helena would be well situated to re-site the Simonstown naval wireless station (though the cost of so doing would not be negligible). The Indian Ocean islands concerned have refuelling and replenishment stations, and all that is necessary for the storage of the strategic ammunition reserves at Simonstown and Ganspan. (This is another South African arsenal from which the larger part of ammunition reserves have been removed, it is believed, partly for strategic reasons and partly because of the risk of sabotage.)

7. Another relevant factor is that the usefulness of Simonstown has been greatly diminished by the scrapping of troopships. With regard to costs, recent improvements in mobile replenishment and the increase in 'float support' ships make it possible for the Royal Navy to give up the Simonstown rights.

8. Beyond this, naval thinking no longer considers the Cape route itself to be vital in the sense it was thought to be in the Second World War. It is widely questioned whether convoys would be sent round the Cape in a major war when the Western powers and the Soviet Union might be bombarding each other with nuclear weapons. There is, however, a difference of strategic opinion on this point, and the Cape sea route would remain important in any conventional war east of Suez, during which little reliance could be placed on the Suez Canal. The present operations in defence of Malaysia are a case in point. This point, therefore, needs to be examined further.

[1] Official Report, col. 1419.

B. *Future Strategic Needs*

9. The Indian Ocean is an area of instability that is likely to need for a decade or more an Amphibious Warfare Squadron with at least a two-brigade lift and with a division (three brigades) of troops attached. Practical and political arguments favour such a force being British; the Pentagon concurs.

10. Such a force would need some sort of naval base facilities within the Indian Ocean area. A distinction must be made between a *main base*, like Portsmouth or Singapore, and a *'forward operating base'*, like Simonstown and the naval facilities in Aden. The Royal Navy in Singapore directly employs 10,000 people. If Singapore was lost to us, the Royal Navy would either have to use Fremantle as a main base, or else have only forward operating bases within the Indian Ocean. Simonstown employs only 100 Royal Navy officers and ratings ashore. This is some measure of the fact that it is only a base of the 'forward operating' kind, i.e. it can be used for refuelling, harbouring depot ships and as a local headquarters and wireless station.

11. Over the next five to ten years, amphibious task forces are likely to increase in range and duration (increased displacement; nuclear propulsion, etc.), which means that Simonstown need not be ruled out as a place for supporting operations in, say, the Bay of Bengal. However, other possibilities exist in addition to Singapore:

(a) *Aden*. British sovereignty insecure, but economic pressure likely to induce Aden to agree to continuing leasehold arrangements.

(b) *Diego Suarez in Mauritius*. Mauritius used by Transport Command already. Independence unlikely to affect arrangements.

(c) *Aldabra Atoll in Seychelles*. Good for small and medium size ships. Air-strip to be developed by R.A.F. Transport Command.

(d) *Karachi* (on leasehold basis). Is already used by the Royal Navy to a considerable extent for minor repairs.

(e) *Australia*. The only ultimately secure base east of Suez. Opportunity for developing base facilities.

12. For an amphibious task force no naval arrangements are really useful unless also facilities for training troops ashore. Such exist in Western Australia, but not in South Africa. Indeed, wisely, the base at Fremantle is *already* being extensively developed for this purpose.

C. *Air Facilities*

13. Though not involving the Simonstown Agreement, Mr Louw's threat gave rise to renewed examination of the problems which the Royal Air Force might have to face, as it occasionally applies for and receives permission to over-fly South Africa for trooping and air reinforcement operations.

14. At present there are three alternative air routes to points east of Suez, of which the first is about to be terminated (El Adem), and the second is of doubtful durability.

(*a*) From Libya, across the Sudan to Aden;

(*b*) From Cyprus, across Turkey, Persia and Pakistan which, like Great Britain, are members of CENTO;

(*c*) The so-called 'Westabout' route across Canada to Vancouver and thence across the Pacific. This is feasible for the new R.A.F. transport 'plane, the *Belfast*, which has a range of up to 3,500 miles.[1]

D. *Conclusion*

15. When this Appendix was prepared, as part of the Working Party's investigation during the first part of 1964, it concluded:

> There is no reason why Great Britain should take the initiative in terminating the Simonstown Agreement, in spite of the view of many strategists that present joint defence arrangements under the Agreement have become largely a matter of advantage to South Africa. Britain is seen as paying a high political price in terms of jeopardizing the good will of the non-white members of the Commonwealth and of the rest of Africa for an asset which is strategically expendable.

> If South Africa were to terminate the Simonstown Agreement, either because she did not receive the Buccaneers, or for any other reason, such as economic sanctions imposed by the United Nations and complied with by the United Kingdom, then the strategic loss could be compensated without undue difficulty.

> The criterion of judgment is that Simonstown is useful but not of irreplaceable strategic importance.

16. In November, 1964, the South African Prime Minister publicly threatened to cancel the Simonstown Agreement unless the Buccaneer aircraft under order were delivered. This threat—which had no legal justification, as 'planes did not form part of the Agreement—did not, however, account for the Government's decision to supply the 16 Buccaneers, for which substantial advance payments had been made. This decision was chiefly motivated by the principle of maintaining contracts, especially at a time of grave balance of payments difficulties. The Government considered the only justification for annulling the contract would have been if the 'planes had been urgently needed for the British armed forces. As they were not, it was decided that the initial order—but not its complement of 14 further 'planes—should be delivered.[2]

[1] Though to reach the Persian Gulf this route takes too long to be militarily desirable.

[2] See additional note on page 170.

17. Following Dr Verwoerd's threat, the Prime Minister, the Rt. Hon. Harold Wilson, MP, commented on its implications for the value of the Simonstown base in the following terms:

If Dr Verwoerd thinks that the Simonstown Agreement can be broken off by the South African Government in this way because they are annoyed about some action we have taken in conformity with our obligations to the United Nations, it will cast doubts in the minds of many hon. Members on what the value of this base would, after all, be in a war if South Africa disapproved of Britain's action in entering that war.

(Official Report, 17th November, 1964.)

XIV · THE UNION OF SOUTH AFRICA OF 1910 AND THE FEDERAL PRINCIPLE

1. The federal principle is that of the co-ordinate division of powers, that is to say, dividing the powers in a written constitution in such a way that both the central and the regional governments are, each within their own defined sphere, co-ordinate and independent.[1]

2. This the Constitution of the Union of South Africa of 1910 never was.[2] It cannot therefore be said that federation has already been tried in South Africa and found wanting. From the beginning, by deliberate decision, the four provincial governments were *subordinate* to, not co-ordinate with, the central (if peripatetic) Government of Pretoria/Cape Town. When the self-governing colonies of the Cape, Natal, the Orange River and the Transvaal united, they established a parliament for the whole Union and four elective councils, one for each of the uniting colonies, now provinces of the Union. These provincial councils were empowered to make ordinances on a list of subjects set out in the Constitution, which included education (other than higher education), agriculture, municipal institutions, roads and hospitals. These ordinances were subject to the approval of the Union Government, and were valid only in so far as they did not conflict with an act of the Union Parliament. That Parliament from the beginning had power to override the provincial councils at any time—or to abolish them altogether.

3. This was not haphazard occurrence. When the delegates of the four colonies met in 1909 to draw up the Constitution, there were

[1] Cp. Sir Robert Garron's definition quoted in the *Report of the Royal Commission on the Australian Constitution*, 1929, p. 230: 'A form of government in which sovereignty or political power is divided between the central and local governments, so that each of them within its own sphere is independent of the other.'

[2] Cp. W. P. M. Kennedy and H. J. Scholssberg, *Law and Custom of the South African Constitution*.

long debates as to whether the federal or unitary principle should be followed. The Natal delegates were in favour of a federal system. But the others preferred the centralizing principle.[1] How important this was in relation to the racial questions was well brought out by one of the framers of the Constitution, the late Lionel Curtis, in a letter to *The Times* in 1951:

'Lord Brand speaks of the South African constitution as a "federal constitution". He at any rate should know that it was not. The Selbourne memorandum had assumed that the constitution of South Africa must be federal like that of the United States of America, Canada and Australia. Lord Selbourne accordingly instructed Sir William Marris, afterwards Finance Minister of India, and myself to suggest what powers should be vested in the Union Government and what other powers should be reserved to the States. In a federation the federal Government is forbidden to interfere with powers reserved to the States. Sir William Marris and I had no hesitation in allotting the control of native affairs, that is to say the relations of whites and coloured people, to the federal Government. We were no less clear that the control of education should be reserved to the States as in the United States of America, Canada and Australia.

'Now education raised the question of the relations of white and coloured people in its acutest form. For the Government which controls education must decide whether white and coloured children are to be educated in separate schools or are to be mixed in the same school. It was thus apparent that the federal Government could not control the relations of white and coloured children if the control of education was reserved to the Governments of the States. We then saw that every department of life in South Africa raised the question of the mutual relations of white and coloured people. No constitution would work in South Africa which forbade the central Government to control all the varied relations of white to coloured people. The constitution must empower the central Government to control the provincial Governments and therefore to alter their powers at will. In other words, the Government of South Africa must be unitary.

'Generals Botha and Smuts were at once convinced by this argument. They therefore advised the adoption of a unitary constitution, and their advice was accepted.'

4. If federation is to be relevant today in South Africa, it must be true federation, with the federal principle applied racially as well as politically. In other words, all South Africans must desire to be united but not unitary. If they are unprepared even for this, then partition or

[1] Cp. Sir E. H. Walton, *The Inner History of the National Convention of South Africa.*

subjugation (by whites as at present, or by Africans in the future) are the only possible alternatives.

XV · THE PATTERN OF SOUTH AFRICAN TRADE

1. South Africa—a term which for trade purposes includes the High Commission Territories and South-West Africa—typically imports more goods by value than she exports. The gap is more than made up by gold production, which generally leaves South Africa with a favourable trade balance (including gold). However, the net payments for services— insurance, freight, banking, tourism—are adverse. Before and immediately after the war the balance on current account was generally unfavourable, a net inflow of capital arriving each year to balance this. The big change in recent years is that the net movement of capital has changed from inward to outward, whether under exchange control or not. In the last decade exports and gold production have both risen formidably, and in 1962, with their help, South Africa was able not only to pay for services, but to send abroad R75 million of private capital and to increase gold reserves by the remarkable sum of R188 million. In 1963 these trends continued; reserves, at the end of October, were at a record level of R516 million, and gold production reached the all-time peak of 2,344 million fine ounces in that month. The capital outflow has continued, roughly half consisting of overseas-held capital (mostly British) being repatriated, half by net exports of South African capital outside the Republic. Imports have been allowed to expand by more than a quarter. Exports have shown some slackening in the previous rate of increase; in the earlier part of 1963 they were running behind 1962, but by September 1963 their value for the first nine months of the year had edged slightly ahead of the corresponding value in 1962.

External Trade of South Africa and Dependencies

Year	Imports* c.i.f.	Exports* f.o.b.	Gold output*	Increase* in gold holdings
1960	1111	884	500	−43
1961	1005	952	575	86
1962	1027	945	637	143
1962 Jan.–Sep.	747	716	314a	95a
1963 Jan.–Sep.	887	734	431a	71a

a = January–June.   * Figures in millions of Rand.
(Source: S.A. Reserve Bank Quarterly Bulletin.)

Increase in Self-sufficiency
2. Thus South Africa has become one of the few natural capital-exporting countries of the world, partly owing to the chance that no

new major gold-mining discovery has been made to absorb the mounting funds available. The Government's aim is to use these resources for its aim of economic independence (the National Party, unlike South African business, has always thought in terms of siege), but faces a certain unwillingness to invest on the part of businessmen. Paradoxically, this investment-shyness keeps the present boom from inflationary dangers. Investment is at last now rising, not least on the part of foreign firms who are forced into 'defensive investment' in local factories in order to preserve their existing markets. This pattern, set by the Government's planned use of import and capital exchange controls, is not peculiar to South Africa; but South Africa has the advantage of being able to offer cheap and plentiful finance.

3. Self-sufficiency is being pushed ahead fast, particularly in the fields of textile and clothing manufacture, vehicle and arms manufacture, chemicals and most recently, aircraft.

Imports

4. The import list is typically that of a developed country, with the emphasis on machinery and manufactures, except that South Africa produces many of her raw materials within her own borders as well as most of her food, and thus is far less reliant on import trade than, for instance, Great Britain. She is also self-sufficient in coal, but not in oil, though at Sasolburg (SASOL) in the Free State a government company operates the largest oil-from-coal process in the world. In the first seven months of 1963, imports totalled 221 million gallons of motor spirit (218 million gallons last year, in the corresponding seven months), 104 million gallons (88 million) of gas oil, 268 million gallons (225 million gallons) of crude oil, and smaller amounts of heavy diesel oil, paraffin and lubricating oil. In order of importance, sources were Iran, Aden refinery, Bahrein, Saudi Arabia, the Dutch Antilles, Sabah in Malaysia, Kuwait and Venezuela.[1]

5. Main suppliers to South Africa in the seven months of all types of goods were: Britain (30·6 per cent), the U.S.A. (16·5 per cent), Western Germany (10·4 per cent), Japan (4·7 per cent), Canada (3·8 per cent), Italy and Iran (3 per cent), France (2·7 per cent), Netherlands, Rhodesia, Sweden, Switzerland, Congo-Leo, Pakistan, Ceylon. Only in the last two cases is there any political significance in this list; South Africa cannot buy tea and jute from India because of the trade ban, which Pakistan does not apply.

Exports

6. *The list of exports demonstrates South Africa's great natural resistance to boycott. Most of the commodities enter a world market in which it*

[1] Cp. Appendix XVII below for a more detailed consideration of the oil question.

would be impracticable to discriminate against a South African product.
The most susceptible to boycott methods would appear to be consumer
goods, mainly fruit, fish, wine, which represents about 10 per cent of the
total, and South Africa's small but (until recently) growing trade in
manufactured goods, mainly to the Federation, the rest of Africa, and
the Indian Ocean area.

Main Exports, January-September 1963

Commodity	1962 R.mn.	1963 R.mn.	Percentage change
Wool	69·5	72·5	+ 4
Maize	55·0	64·7	+18
Fruit	63·2	63·4	+ 1
Diamonds	52·3	64·0	+22
Prescribed materials (uranium)	54·9	51·3	− 7
Sugar	22·0	27·1	+23
Wine (January–July)	16·5	21·7	+31
Hides and skins	19·2	21·1	+10
Copper	13·1	20·9	+59
Asbestos	18·8	17·6	− 6
Fish	18·5	16·8	− 9
Ferro alloys	7·6	10·6	+39
Lead	8·3	8·2	− 1
Wood pulp	7·1	8·0	+13
Manganese	8·9	7·8	−13
Mining machinery	6·9	6·4	− 7
Wattle bark and extract	5·8	6·0	+ 3
Pig iron and steel ingots	7·9	5·7	−28
Chrome ore	3·8	2·8	−26
Total (including others)	715·6	733·6	+25

7. Only one of these commodities, fish, can be said to have been
affected by political boycott in the year to September 1963. The market
for fishmeal and tinned pilchards in the Philippines from the South-
West African coasts has suffered from a decline which was partly political. Elsewhere exporters of men's and women's clothing, footwear, glass
bottles, cheese, biscuits, blankets, paints, polishes, cardboard boxes,
stationery and other sundries sold mainly to the rest of Africa have felt
a decided retrenchment in trade this year. Sales have undoubtedly suffered
from the boycott of Uganda and Tanganyika, and will suffer from that of
Kenya and Kuwait. However, the fall from 1962, which looks to be
about an average 10 per cent, is more than accounted for by the fall in
sales in the chief market, in the Rhodesias and Nyasaland, which is not
political, but is due to the elements of economic recession in those areas,
especially Southern Rhodesia.

8. The export total of these products of secondary industry is not
important. The largest single items are the group 'books, paper and
stationery', R2·7 million (R3·2 million in 1962), men's clothing and
footwear, both R0·8 million (down from R1·2 million). There have been

minor increases in exports of drugs and blasting fuses, up from R0·5 to R0·6 million in each case, but the general trend is plainly downhill. Mr Oppenheimer has said recently that at present there is more scope for investment in the rest of Africa than for exports there.

9. In order of importance, South Africa's customers in the first seven months of 1963 were: Britain, 34·3 per cent; Rhodesia and Nyasaland, 8·5 per cent; U.S.A., 7·9 per cent; Japan, 6·1 per cent; Italy, 4·9 per cent; Western Germany, 4·9 per cent; Belgium, 4·2 per cent; France, 3 per cent; Netherlands, 2·3 per cent. Britain's leading position is partly due to the existence of world commodity markets in London. The rest of Africa outside the Rhodesias took 3·9 per cent, which was a decrease from 4·3 per cent last year. There were notable increases in South African sales to Britain, West Germany, Australia and Belgium among developed countries, and also to Eire, Senegal, Kuwait, South Vietnam, Switzerland. A remarkable new export trade has opened up to China (no details in the monthly statistics) and Albania (R649,000 of exports against nil in 1962). Exports to Portuguese territories in Africa, 1·8 per cent of the total, were unchanged.

10. African markets outside the Federation and the Portuguese territories took only 2·5 per cent of the Republic's total exports in the first seven months of 1962, and this dropped to about 2 per cent in the first seven months of 1963. Asian markets outside Japan, Hong Kong and Turkey took only 2·8 per cent and 2·9 per cent respectively, while exports to Communist Europe represented about 1 per cent in each year. *The effect of a total Afro-Asian-Communist boycott, excluding these countries, might cut about 6 per cent of South Africa's export trade. However, its actual effect at present, owing to its not being applied and to the re-export of re-labelled South African goods via Southern Rhodesia, is at most 1.7 per cent.*

Effects of a Boycott on Consumer Goods

11. One recourse of a government faced with a decline in sales of South Africa's secondary industry would be to step up purchasing power at home, which has long been the plea of secondary industry itself; in fact, it might be justifiable to urge the boycott of such goods on the ground that it would be likely to benefit the non-white buying public. To a lesser extent, this would also be the first response to an effective boycott of South Africa's agricultural consumer goods. Maize and sugar exports in particular consist of surpluses left over after home demand, in each case growing, has been satisfied. Fruit, fish and wine, in the event of not achieving sales abroad, would meet a rather less elastic demand at home.

12. Another by-product might be the development of separate markets outlets for goods from the Territories, at present marketed as

South African, to their benefit. This might particularly help Swaziland sugar and citrus fruit, Basutoland wool and mohair. Indeed, it might be assumed that South African capital would pour into Swaziland to its benefit, to take advantage of the freedom from boycott which that country would enjoy. Swazi oranges are already being marketed under their own label. These economic facts are relevant to any evaluation of the implications of the recent Swaziland elections.

XVI · THE UNITED KINGDOM'S ECONOMIC STAKE IN SOUTH AFRICA

Its Nature

I. *Trade*

1. In 1963 the U.K. trade with South Africa (excluding South-West Africa) represented *4·8 per cent of total British exports*, and 2·4 per cent of total imports. *This, however, represented 30 per cent of South Africa's total imports.*[1]

(a) *Exports: Total in* 1963: £187·8 *million* (excluding gold).
The main commodities exported to South Africa were:

Product	% of the Exports (in this sector)	£ million
Transport equipment (mainly motor cars)	8·3	52·2
Machinery (not electrical)	5·0	42·6
Electrical machinery	7·2	22·9
Textiles	6·3	16·0

(b) *Imports: Total in* 1963: £166·2 *million*.
The main imported items were the following:

Product	% of the Imports (in this sector)	£ million
Fruit and vegetables	11·9	33·4
Maize	11·8	14·0
Sugar	5·9	10·2
Textile fibres (mainly wool)	4·8	12·8

[1] For other suppliers, see text of the Study Report, para. 108.

II. *Invisible Earnings*

2.

Item	£ million	
	1961	1962
Freight and insurance	20·0	15·5
Other transport	7·5	7·5
Travel	9·5	9·0
Government and other services	11·5	13·5
Investment income	62·5	56·0

III. *Investments*

3. The Board of Trade figures published in November 1963 indicate direct British investment in South Africa of £219 million, excluding oil, banking and insurance. To the figure of £219 million should be added non-direct U.K. investments of £250 million; U.K.-owned companies registered in South Africa, £80 million; and current liabilities, £280 million. This total of £789 million may be compared with the figure of £1,000 million given in the report of the U.N. Expert Committee (see text of the Report, para. 45). Oil, banking and insurance figures could reasonably account for the difference.

4. American figures derived from the South Africa Reserve Bank give the following distribution of the investment at the end of 1960 in comparison with those of the U.S.A.:

	Millions of dollars	
	U.K.	U.S.A.
Mining	736	182
Manufacturing	682	113
Insurance and finance	420	50
Commerce	350	78
Other	155	63
Public authorities	175	355
Total	2,159	822
% of total foreign investment in S. Africa.	58	19

The total U.K. investment stake in South Africa may be taken as being between £900 and £1,000 million.

Effect of Total U.N. Trade Sanctions

5. The Christian decision for or against such trade sanctions must be based on moral considerations. If they are considered right, they must be followed, at whatever economic cost to this country. If they are considered wrong, they must be opposed, regardless of the economic advantage this country may thereby continue for a period to acquire.

6. However, it is necessary to estimate the magnitude of the losses

involved, and whether there would be any particular areas of hardship.

7. Equally relevant is the contention that the losses would be temporary, being limited to the period of the sanctions. As against this, the possible alternatives of increasing sabotage and eventual racial war suggest the possibility of much heavier—and definitive—losses.

8. Any action could be envisaged only as part of a U.N. operation, observed by all other member states, which would necessitate a naval blockade, at least of the main ports, for a considerable period of time. In this hypothesis, losses to the country would be the following:

I. *Exports*

9. The figures for exports given above represent one-sixtieth of the gross domestic product, and employment of some 150,000 people. Some of the goods could be exported to other countries, but some losses would certainly occur. For instance—to take the case of the items representing the highest percentage of total U.K. exports in a given undertaking—the loss of overseas car sales (where exports account for a quarter of total production) would amount to some 2 per cent.

10. How could these losses be compensated? One method would be to provide compensation for all firms which suffered a loss of more than a given percentage of their export earnings. In the years 1959-1961 the number of cases which would have been involved if the cut-off level were 20 per cent was 52, involving £136 million worth of business; if the level were 10 per cent there would have been a further 272 cases, representing an annual loss of £51·3 million.

11. Another proposal is that the goods involved should be sent to underdeveloped countries, with loans financed by the U.K. herself. If this were done by concerted U.N. action, it would avoid exacerbated competition in alternative markets, by developing a new market in the underdeveloped countries equivalent in size to the South African.

II. *Employment*

12. Most of the 150,000 who would be potentially redundant as a result of this loss of exports could be absorbed at a time of full employment, though there would be some significant pockets of unemployment, e.g. Southampton.

III. *Investments*

13. The income from these would be lost, amounting to some £60 million per year.

14. Professor G. D. N. Worswick has suggested the following with regard to compensation for forfeited investment income:

> The easiest, technically, is investment income, which on our supposition is to be cut off. The British Government would offer

to take title of all shares and bonds concerned, and pay compensation, in the form of interest-bearing British government securities. The interest on these securities could be financed during the ban by an increase in the income tax on unearned incomes. If, when the ban is over, the South African investments begin to yield again, the money will flow into the Treasury, and the U.K. taxpayer can be relieved *pro tanto*.

IV. *Imports*

15. These are chiefly agricultural, and could be replaced by other sources of supply. There might be some difficulty in respect of sugar, and oranges would not be available in certain months.

V. *Gold*

16. Gold is a special case. In 1959-61 the U.K. imported just under one-half of her total gold imports from South Africa, amounting to some £230 million per annum. But this gold is not placed in reserves, but on the London bullion market. It is then re-exported. Thus during the same three years, average gold exports amounted to £290 million. In other words, the only special problem for the U.K. would be the bullion brokers who would lose an important commission.

17. The gold issue is really one of international liquidity. World gold reserves are sufficient to survive without South African gold for a long period, whether or not the opportunity of the cessation of South African gold supplies were seized to demonetize gold internationally, as it already is internally.

VI. *Balance of Payments*

18. The loss to the U.K. balance of payments would be somewhere between the £60 million from dividends and the £250 million from visible and invisible trade combined. The upper figure would depend on the elasticity of other export markets. If the loss were total, it could amount to £5 per head of the population, which would have to be met by reducing imports. If the Government tried to hold back the whole economy, as they have done in recent years whenever imports have exceeded exports, it could mean reducing the G.N.P. by £600 million to save imports of £200 million. In this extreme case, sanctions against South Africa could cost Britain $2\frac{1}{2}$ per cent of her national product.

19. This, however, assumes unilateral action by the U.K. In the context of a U.N. operation, measures could be taken to prevent any country suffering disproportionately (e.g. I.M.F. credits).

Conclusions

20. Given a reasonable rate of growth, *in the context of a concerted U.N. operation*, Britain's overall loss could be relatively slight. But

balance of payments difficulties would make it a difficult political decision.

21. Britain's decision, however, would be decisive, as her trade constitutes one-third of the total external trade of South Africa.

XVII · OIL SANCTIONS

1. South Africa is much less dependent on oil than European countries. The reason for this is the immense resources of cheap coal, which provide 87 per cent of South Africa's total energy requirements. The whole country is consciously geared to a minimum dependence on oil, and maximum dependence on a coal-burning railway system. Most factories are powered by electricity extracted from coal, or by coal itself.

2. At most, therefore, sanctions could affect the remaining 13 per cent of South Africa's energy requirements. These are derived from oil, from the following sources (1962 figures):

	Per cent
Domestic production from coal (SASOL)	5
Crude oil imports	36
Product imports	59

The most important petroleum product is motor gasoline, which accounts for 56·3 per cent of the oil consumed. It is particularly important for internal airways, private motor-cars, agriculture[1] and the mobile defence forces.

3. This at first sight presents considerable vulnerability; but it must be assumed the South African government would take resolute action to counter the effects of any oil sanctions. The following are among the measures which would be open to them.

(a) Supply

4. There are at present some four months' reserves stocked in South Africa (two months' commercial reserves, seven weeks' strategic reserve). This figure could be increased to perhaps one year's supplies by intensive stock-piling: there would be plenty of warning that international sanctions might be imposed.

5. The present SASOL plant has a capacity of some 300,000 tons of oil, out of a total oil consumption of 3,500,000 tons. By a resolute effort, within two years it is conceivable that two new SASOL plants could be built by South African engineers, at a cost of £60,000,000 each.[2]

---

[1] In 1959 there were 106,000 tractors, 45,000 lorries and 80,000 other vehicles on farms in South Africa. Not only are many white farms fairly mechanized, but road transport is the farmer's means of bringing his products to the railhead.

[2] The first SASOL plant cost £110,000,000, but that figure includes amortization charges, and also paying for several costly technical mistakes in the construction.

Indigenous petrol supplies could thus be increased from 10 per cent to 30 per cent of present requirements.

6. Angola[1] produces 1,500,000 tons of crude oil, of which she exports one million tons through the harbour of Luanda, which is only 1,800 miles from Cape Town. A complete blockade of Angola as well as South Africa could be answered by a pipe-line, though this would take 12-15 months to construct across the difficult terrain. (A trunk road to the Angolan border is part of the Odendaal proposals.) It also assumes that Portugal would be prepared to confiscate Petrofina's share of the Angolan oil holdings and export to South Africa in defiance of the United Nations in a sector where she herself is dependent on imports (1,900,000 tons in 1962).

(b) Consumption

7. The immediate introduction of rationing, with priority for the mobile defence and police forces and special allocations for agriculture. At the expense of the private motorist, consumption could be cut by perhaps one-third. Some alleviation of this—but not substantial— could be obtained by private motorists installing producer gas or coal gas fuel equipment in their cars. The large towns could use methane from sewage for their municipal vehicles.

(c) New oil discoveries

8. It cannot be excluded that present intensive oil prospecting within South Africa, and especially in northern Natal and to a lesser extent in South-West Africa, may not result in the discovery of substantial indigenous supplies. A new State Corporation has been set up to develop strategic mineral resources with an initial budget of £7,500,000. The most modern seismic equipment has recently been assembled by the Geological Survey in Pretoria, and three of the world's most prominent oil men have been specially recruited from the U.S.A.—Mr John Mecom, Mr W. P. Blair and Dr Francis Henson (who has been appointed as master of operations). Dr Henson is at present directing the survey of the sea-bed in the Mossel Bay area.

9. When all these factors are taken into account, it is reasonable to envisage that *South Africa could survive the total cessation of sea-borne oil imports for at least two years, and indefinitely if Angolan supplies were available. To assume a total international blockade sustained for so long a period is unrealistic. Therefore oil sanctions by themselves fail as a proposition for coercing a resolute South African government.*

10. The lesson of oil does not stop there: the word 'blockade' requires substantiation. In 1962 South Africa imported 34 million barrels of oil. World exports were 5,000 million barrels. Any one of twenty

[1] 'Angolan oil could save South Africa' was a headline in the *Johannesburg Star* in August 1964.

K

countries could render the blockade ineffective by diverting only a small proportion of their present exports. The commercial incentive for so doing would be eno_mous. At present there is such a glut of petrol that the major refineries are selling more petrol in bulk to small independent competitors, which market it at cut price in competition with their own chains, than South Africa's total requirements. This is an economic situation which defies all government action, except physical controls. Even assuming all governments and the major companies co-operated, there remain the independent suppliers who would stand to gain enormous fortunes. Even a world-wide system of U.N. rationing with inspection would provide no guarantee. So one is forced to the following conclusion: *effective oil sanctions would require to be enforced by a full-scale naval blockade of South Africa for a period of at least two years.*

Note on Oil Sanctions from the Point of View of the Oil Companies
'The proposed oil embargo is explicitly aimed at achieving a political objective. A new element in the eighteen-year-old United Nations dis-dispute is that Afro-Asian and Allied delegations now realize that eight countries (United States, United Kingdom, France, Germany, Italy, Netherlands, Belgium and Japan) together account for 70 per cent of South Africa's external trade and that economic sanctions to be effective require the active support of South Africa's main trading partners.

'Accordingly, protagonists of a boycott have been deploying strength with some success in manoeuvring important trading partners like the United States and the United Kingdom into a position where they may have to choose between South Africa and the rest of Africa.

'It is thought that if those states pressing for a boycott of oil supplies failed to get satisfaction within the United Nations, they may carry the struggle outside the world organization and use other means to continue the campaign against South Africa's policies of racial discrimi-nation, possibly boycotting in their own countries international corpora-tions which trade in South Africa. It is unnecessary to emphasize how such a threat could jeopardize the interests of international oil com-panies.

'Although oil industry members are far from complacent about the long-term solution to the problem, some of the tensions in the shorter term may be easing. For example, both Iran and Venezuela, who understand the oil business, have said in the General Assembly that, however much they find themselves in sympathy with the anti-apartheid movement, they are not prepared individually to embargo oil supplies. Furthermore, present indications are that considerable difficulty would be encountered in securing support for any Security Council resolution recommending an oil embargo.

'It is also significant that, although speakers in the United Nations have been advocating an embargo supported by OPEC and have stated openly that without OPEC support it might fail, no such formal recommendation has been made by the Assembly, nor to the best of our knowledge has OPEC made any formal decision to support an embargo.

'Seventy-five developing countries (over thirty African states among them) subscribed to the declaration on trade and development adopted unanimously by the General Assembly on 11th November 1963, which, among other things, supported the principle that obstacles to the flow of international trade can be not only harmful to the countries concerned but also to world prosperity.

'The declaration envisaged the growth and development of international trade as a key to the economic development of the developing countries. With these principles all international corporations would be in agreement, because as international commercial operators they believe in the expansion of international trade, and their paramount aim is to maintain their commercial interests in any part of the world, as far as their resources and commitments elsewhere may allow.

'In view of the many possibilities which exist, it is difficult for an international oil company to declare at this stage how it might react in any hypothetical situation, but it would be quite ready to define its position in terms of the principle, i.e. as a commercial operator it cannot take sides in any political dispute.

'A spokesman for a major oil company has given these specific answers to the following questions:

1. Q. Who supplies oil to South Africa?
   A. Shell and B.P., Compagnie Française des Pétroles (C.F.P.) and the two American companies, Caltex and Mobil.
2. Q. Who could supply oil to South Africa?
   A. Past history has shown that a universal boycott is difficult to achieve, and there is always the problem of small independent operators in the United States, the Japanese, or certain of the producing companies who have government-owned marketing organizations.
3. Q. Which of the countries now supplying oil is constitutionally in a position to stop the supply?
   A. I think it is fair to say that all of the companies currently marketing in South Africa would not wish to supply if requested not to do so by their home governments, whether or not that government was constitutionally set up to request such embargo.
4. Q. Has, for instance, the President of the United States such power, or would he need to go to Congress? Would the British Government need to seek parliamentary authority or does the Executive

already have the necessary authority under existing statute law?
A. These have the same answer really as question No. 3.
5. Q. What would be the effect on British and American companies?
A. The scale of the Shell/B.P. investment in South Africa is approximately £45 million. If a real boycott were effective, the direct effect on British investments would be related to the sum of approximately £1,000 million, which we understand is invested by British interests in South Africa.
6. Q. What would be the effect on the South African economy?
A. The South African economy, which at the moment is booming, would in the end grind to a halt if a total embargo were effective, and no alternative indigenous sources of supply were discovered and developed.
7. Q. What stocks of oil does South Africa hold at present?
A. The stockholding is related to commercial market requirements, and normally represents about two months' consumption.'[1]

XVIII · FINANCIAL AID FOR THE VICTIMS OF APARTHEID

The Sources of Aid

1. It may be helpful to clarify the various sources of aid available.

(*a*) Christian Action (2 Amen Court, London, E.C.4) is responsible for a Defence and Aid Fund. This is for legal defence and welfare, and Christian Action mainly chooses its own objects of help, e.g. the Treason Trial (1959-62); the Rivonia Trial. It passes some money to Defence and Aid in South Africa.

(*b*) Defence and Aid in South Africa is a separate organization from (*a*), with its headquarters in Johannesburg. It also deals with legal defence. Because of limited funds it has had to hand over welfare and relief in Johannesburg to other bodies.

(*c*) Money for relief and welfare is being provided:

(i) By the Division of Inter-Church Aid, Refugee and World Service of the W.C.C. in Geneva, and is channelled through the Christian Council of South Africa to various centres. In Cape Town the work is done by a Co-ordinating Committee; other places receiving help are Durban, Pietermaritzburg, etc.

(ii) By the Friends Service Council. This is administered for Johannesburg by the Quaker Service Fund, by a social worker seconded from the Friends Service Council.

[1] In addition there is a strategic reserve of a further two months' supply.

The Work of Defence and Aid in South Africa

2. Between November 1963 and June 1964, Defence and Aid handled 23 cases and 5 appeals in the Johannesburg area:

Total number of accused	83
Number against whom charges were withdrawn	17
Number sentenced	38
Number acquitted	3
Escaped	1
Committed to mental institution	23

In 3 appeals, involving 40 people, appeals of 39 were dismissed, and 1 sentence was set aside. It is certain that sentences would have been imposed, where cases were withdrawn or acquittal obtained, had no legal defence been available.

3. The Cape Town office of Defence and Aid, during the first six months this year, accepted a total of 9 cases involving 95 persons, and 10 appeals involving 62 persons. Of the 5 cases which have been completed, there have been 21 convictions and 15 acquittals. Twenty people have been released from gaol sentences on appeal, 15 have had fines reduced and 5 have received reduced sentences.

Some Individual Cases

4. The flavour of 90-day Clause proceedings is best judged from individual cases. The following three occurred recently:

(a) John Molefe

John Molefe spent almost three months—from May to August 1963 —as a 90-day detainee in solitary confinement. He was released from detention without being charged. In November 1963 he was served with banning orders. The orders contained a clause forbidding him to enter factory premises. However, Molefe did not realize that this clause applied to him, as a *labourer*, in the factory where he worked. Nor did he understand that he was, in fact, being severed from his livelihood. After the Christmas holidays he returned to the factory as usual, and there he was arrested. Molefe was charged with breaking his banning orders, and sentenced to 18 months' imprisonment, with 12 months suspended. Before he could serve his sentence, the old man became ill; soon after he came out of gaol, pending appeal, he died. His wife has since been served with banning orders.

(b) Looksmart Solwandle

One of the most important cases handled by the Fund during 1963-64 was the inquest held into the death—suicide by hanging—of a 90-day detainee, Looksmart Solwandle. In the course of this case, the whole question of the treatment of 90-day detainees was brought into open court. One of the witnesses, Mr Isaac Tlale, described how he had been given electric shocks after refusing to give evidence for the state. After his arms and legs had been secured, a bag was placed over his head, and he was then shocked into unconsciousness.

(c) Mrs Lettie Sibeko

Mrs Lettie Sibeko, who had spent her entire pregnancy in gaol (including five months in solitary confinement), was granted £100 bail shortly before the birth of her child, after urgent application. Three attorneys had to work on this case; the briefing of two counsels was necessary.

5. If the provision of adequate legal defence is essential, the provision of relief for the families of the detained is imperative. Thus one of those condemned to life imprisonment at the Rivonia trial leaves behind seven children. The mother has just begun her second 90-day detention. The grandmother is attempting to care for the infants, and is destitute.

Action in this Country

6. Legal advice and defence; relief for the dependants of political prisoners and 90-day detainees; aid for refugees—are all different, but all three should be the objects of Christian giving. The World Council of Churches has recently appealed for $1,000,000 for current emergencies in Africa, which includes such relief and aid. In these islands it is the Christian Aid Department of the British Council of Churches which must raise the money; it has already sent a first contribution.

XIX · THE RESPECT OF THE MANDATE IN SOUTH-WEST AFRICA

Area and Population

1. South-West Africa measures 318,099 miles in extent, and is larger than France and Great Britain put together. Its total population only slightly exceeds half a million people.

Before 1918

2. South-West Africa became a German colony in 1884. The history of German colonial rule is not relevant to this investigation, save in so far as German colonial practices have contributed to the modern South-West African situation. It lasted until 1915, during which period German governors at first tried to regulate their relationships with the tribes of South-West Africa—the Hereros, the Nama, the Berg-Damara, the Ovambo and the Rehobothers—by treaty, but as each of

the major tribes in turn rose in rebellion against the German colonial rulers, so they were put down by the German army. The Herero war of 1904 illustrates the ferocity with which the German colonial rulers dealt with rebellion. It is estimated that during the war and subsequent to it the Germans were responsible for the extermination of some 65,000 Hereros out of a tribe of 80,000. In addition the survivors lost their tribal lands and their cattle. In 1915 South-West Africa was occupied by South African commandos under General Louis Botha, and from this time until the Treaty of Versailles South-West Africa was under military rule.

3. The correspondence between Generals Smuts and Botha in 1918 shows that they had hoped that South Africa might be allowed to annex South-West Africa at the conclusion of hostilities. At Versailles, however, the former German colony was placed under the control of South Africa as the mandatory power. The bestowal of the mandate did not confer full sovereignty upon South Africa, but only the responsibility of administering South-West Africa in conformity with the principles of the whole mandatory system, in trust for its inhabitants. South-West Africa was classified as a 'C' mandate, which meant that in terms of Article 22 of the Covenant of the League of Nations South Africa was entitled to administer South-West Africa as an integral part of the territory of the mandatory power, subject to safeguards in the interests of the indigenous people, because of the sparseness of the population, its remoteness from the centres of civilization, and because it was contiguous to the mandatory power itself, South Africa. When the Council of the League adopted the actual mandate on 17th December 1920, South Africa was required:

> to promote to the utmost the material and moral wellbeing and the social progress of the inhabitants of the territory (Art. 2).

Art. 7 provided:

> If any dispute whatever should arise between the Mandatory and another member of the League of Nations relating to the interpretation or the application of the provision of the mandate, such dispute, if it cannot be settled by negotiation, shall be submitted to the Permanent Court of International Justice.

The Period of the Mandate

4. After German oppression, the indigenous peoples of the territory hoped for a new era of enlightened administration. They were soon disillusioned. In the first years of the mandate South Africa mounted three punitive expeditions against Chief Mandume of the Ukuanyama (a campaign during which a hundred or more of the Chief's supporters, including the Chief himself, were to be killed by machine-gun fire);

against the Bondelswarts under Abraham Morris (a tribe of the Nama which were bombed by South African aircraft, killing Morris and another hundred men, women and children); and finally, the Rehobothers. At the same time Smuts, seeing South-West Africa as a South African colony, threw the country open to the white settler. A Land Board was set up to allocate farms to new white settlers, and during the first five years of the mandate some 900 large farms had been allocated to settlers. By 1935 the number of farmers had grown to 1,500, who between them owned about one-sixth of the territory's farming land. In 1922 the South African Government had reported that reserves had been selected for the African reserves. The areas set aside are not in African opinion suitable for agriculture, being situated in sand-veld areas where it is difficult to tap underground water because of its depth. In fact, the white farmers hold the major part of the land surface of South-West Africa.

5. During the period of the mandate the Mandates Commission was not idle. It was continually critical of South Africa's reports. The central controversy of the mandate years ranged over the question of who was to pay for development in the territory. The simplest way of establishing how South Africa discharged her duty towards the territory is to examine in turn land distribution, population movement, wages and industry.

Topography

6. The main ranching areas of South-West Africa lie along the plateau within the police zone bounded on the west by the Namib desert—the diamond area—and on the east by the Kalahari desert. Of the scattered reserves within the police zone only the Rehoboth lands are considered to be of agricultural value. The majority of South-West Africa's African population live in the far north beyond the police zone. Ovamboland, which holds half the African population, experiences annual flooding of as much as three-fifths of its area, so that the mound and furrow method of planting has to be used. The Kaokoveld is barren and mountainous and sparsely populated, while in Okavango the population lives mostly along the river.

Population and Land Ownership

7. Since 1913 the European population of South-West Africa has increased from 14,830, owning 1,138 farms measuring 11,490,000 hectares in extent, to approximately 72,000 in 1962, owning some 5,500 farms measuring in extent 39,812,000 hectares.[1] By contrast, in 1962 it was estimated that the total land in the possession of 428,000 Africans and approximately 24,000 Coloureds and Rehobothers amounted to 21,825,997 hectares.[2] Of the 428,000 Africans, only 168,000 live in the

[1] 98·3 million acres.　　　　[2] 53·9 million acres.

police zone. Thus *the Europeans, though only one in seven of the total population, own two-thirds of the land.* In 1952 the average white farm measured 28 square miles in extent. In the police zone approximately 72,300 Europeans farm some 40 million hectares, and 170,000 Africans occupy 6 million hectares approximately.

Wages and Labour

8. From the outset, after recurrent drought South-West Africa's greatest problem has been labour, although the Africans greatly out-number the European farmers, there has been no great enthusiasm to go to the police zone to work on the white farms or in the copper mines. Labour is recruited for mines and farms alike by the South-West African Native Labour Association. Most labour is recruited at the main recruiting centres, Ondangua in Ovamboland and Runtu in the Okavango. Here all labour is classified into those fit for underground work in the mines, those fit for surface mine work or heavy farm labour and those fit only for light farm work such as a shepherd.

9. Each employer pays a capitation fee of £13 per recruit, and the African is thereafter 'required to render his master his service at all fair and reasonable times'. Recruitment proceeds beyond the borders of South-West Africa into Angola, and recruitment is also carried on for South Africa's gold mines.

10. In 1961 over 27,000 Africans were recruited, of which 14,500 came from South-West Africa's northern areas and the remainder from beyond its borders. Of the total number recruited, 8,658 were allocated to South-West African farms, 9,559 to industries and public works, 6,703 to South-West African mines and 2,241 to the South African gold mines. This system of contracted labour maintains in the police zone some 40,000 labourers from the north each year. Wages and terms of work for such labourers in 1962 were as follows:

CATEGORY OF LABOUR	PERIOD OF EMPLOYMENT	WAGE
Mines and industries	309 shifts (working days)	1/9 for first 155 shifts, 2/0 for next 77 shifts, 2/3 for last 77 shifts
Domestic	Twelve months	Upwards of 30/- a month
Farm	12 or 18 months	25/- a month for youngster to £4 a month for a skilled worker.

In addition to these emoluments, labourers receive their keep and shelter. Standards here vary widely from reasonable labour compounds and food on the mines, to farms where no shelter and very poor food is provided.

11. For Africans living within the police zone, this system of contract labour does not apply. Instead, like their counterparts in South Africa, Africans are required to be in possession of a permit to seek work; a permit to be in the area for any purpose other than to seek work; a service contract to prove employment; or, if a schoolboy, a pass to prove his status as such. A failure to produce any of these documents on demand constitutes a criminal offence, and many Africans are fined and imprisoned yearly for these offences.[1] An African in a reserve may not leave it except by permit, or in order to seek for work with a white employer. He cannot buy a railway ticket within the police zone unless he has a pass issued by his employer or a government official. Each reserve, town or farming area becomes for the African, once located there, an island surrounded by a mass of restrictions and laws. If he once steps beyond its bounds without due authority, he is liable to arrest. In addition to the offences listed above, the African may be liable for arrest and imprisonment for entering a location without a permit; unlawful domicile; presence in the police zone without exemption, and failure to pay hut tax.

The Economy of South-West Africa

12. General Smuts told the Fourth Committee of the United Nations at the end of 1946 that South-West Africa had low economic potentialities which, when linked with the backwardness of the vast majority of the people of South-West Africa, made it impossible for him ever to envisage South-West African self-government. Subsequent developments have made it clear that South-West Africa has great economic potentialities. South Africa had initially assumed the deficits incurred during the period of martial law. After assuming the mandate she spent heavily on white settlement. During the thirties a combination of the world depression and a disastrous series of droughts led to a number of deficits in South-West African budgets, all of which were met by South Africa. During this period only diamonds continued to produce revenue, and such resources as the territory possessed were still spent upon the farmers, who brought no increase in revenue by way of return. However, during this period the Karakul sheep was imported from Russia, and immediately thrived in the arid conditions of the territory. Today it forms the backbone of South-West African agricultural wealth. After the Second World War the economy of South-West Africa took a turn for the better. The revenue figure for 1946-47

---

[1] Indeed, as in South Africa, it is difficult for an African to *avoid* periodical fine and/or imprisonment for pass offences. He has only to forget to have it on his person when going 100 yards to a local shop, for instance, and fail to produce it if challenged.

was £2·9 million; for 1956-57, £12 million; and for 1961-62, £15·7 million.

13. The mining industry developed greatly, and in 1961 produced South-West Africa's highest mineral output figure of £26 million (£18 million in diamonds; more than £7 million in base metal exports). Since 1946 South-West Africa has also developed a prosperous fishing industry, based on Walvis Bay.[1] Most of the fish caught are canned or processed, and the Walvis Bay production constitutes 90 per cent of the total output of the fishing industry for South Africa and South-West Africa combined.[2] Agriculture has also extended its activities to dairying and beef cattle.

14. The African in the territory has benefited only peripherally from this economic expansion. The industries which have contributed to this new prosperity are essentially European owned and operated enterprises, in which the role of the African is limited to unskilled labour. Without discussing the details of the African position, it is interesting to note that Dr D. C. Krogh estimated that in 1956 average income per capita was £82·4 per annum (£176·1 in the police zone, and £8·5 outside the police zone).

15. From 1920 to 1948 expenditure from general revenue on Africans in the territory—African tax contributions are not included, as they are paid into Reserve Trust funds—did not exceed 7 per cent of total government expenditure. In 1955 the administration of 'Native Affairs' was switched from Windhoek to Pretoria, and the South African Government took direct control of funds to be spent on Africans. In terms of this arrangement South-West Africa each year pays to the Republic a sum equal to one-fortieth of its expenditure, together with the sum of £50,000. In 1961 this figure was £225,000 which, taken together with the sum voted for African education and health services—still a responsibility for South-West Africa—amounted to a total of £1,430,000 out of estimates for the territory totalling approximately £17 millions.[3]

Education

16. Schools in South-West Africa are largely the result of missionary effort. In 1960, of 93 schools in the police zone, only 10 were government schools. Beyond the zone there were 103 recognized mission schools with 15,000 pupils, and 20 state-subsidized schools with 822 pupils in Ovamboland, with another 10 mission schools in the Okavango. The cost of education as it appears in the South African Year Book for 1958-59 for South-West Africa is as follows:

[1] Walvis Bay is legally part of South Africa, not South-West Africa, as it was a British port during the period of German rule, administered from Cape Town.
[2] Cp. para. 152 (2) in the main body of the report.
[3] This was a year in which an African hospital programme was initiated.

RACE	COST	NUMBER OF SCHOLARS
Europeans (excluding hostel expenses)	£42 19 0	12,740
Coloureds	£24 19 3	(figure not given)
African schools in the police zone	£13 19 4	13,437
African schools outside the police zone	£1 16 2	19,398

17. This report gives some of the relevant figures for South-West Africa during the period it has been a mandate of South Africa. Not all South African statutes apply to South-West Africa, but of recent years, and particularly since South-West Africa became represented in the South African Parliament by virtue of the South-West Africa Affairs Amendment Act of 1949, South African *apartheid* legislation has applied to South-West Africa. The report of the Special Committee of the United Nations in respect of colonial countries refers to the fact that both the General Law Amendment Acts of 1962 and 1963 apply to the territory. Similarly, the Bantu Affairs Act of 1963-64 also applies. Having regard to the duties which were laid upon South Africa by the mandate and are now by the Charter of the United Nations, it is relevant to ask how South Africa has discharged these duties.

The United Nations and South-West Africa

18. In terms of Article 76 of the United Nations Charter, the aims of trusteeship are to further international peace and security; to promote the political and economic, social and educational advancement of the inhabitants of the trust territories, and their progressive development towards self-government or independence as may be appropriate to the particular circumstances of each territory and its people and the freely expressed wishes of the people concerned, and as may be provided by the terms of each trustee agreement; to encourage respect for human rights and fundamental freedoms for all and to encourage recognition of interdependence of the peoples of the world, and to ensure equal treatment in social, economic and commercial matters for all members of the United Nations and their nationals, and equal treatment for the latter in the administration of justice, provided this does not conflict with the attainment of the other objectives of the trusteeship system.

19. When in 1946 the other mandatory powers advised that they were prepared to place their mandated territories under the trusteeship system of the United Nations, South Africa demurred. General Smuts, addressing the Fourth Committee, said that South Africa had a legitimate concern to annex the territory. He stated that South-West Africa was geographically and strategically speaking a part of South Africa, it

was economically dependent upon South Africa, its tribes came from the same racial origins, two-thirds of its whites were South African nationals. He admitted that the fundamental principle of the mandate system and trusteeship was ultimate political self-government and separate statehood, but declared that this was not possible in South-West Africa for the reasons given in paragraph 12. The Fourth Committee decisively rejected Smut's argument, and invited South Africa to submit a trusteeship agreement. This was not done, although in 1946 South Africa submitted a report on her administration of the territory to the United Nations. In 1949, with the Nationalist Government now in power, South Africa announced her inability to comply with the trusteeship resolution, and her decision to submit no more reports or information.

20. The U.N. decided to ask the International Court of Justice for an opinion on the international status of South-West Africa. In July 1950, the Court advised that in its opinion South-West Africa was still a territory held under the international mandate assumed by South Africa in 1920, and it rejected the South African contention that the mandate had lapsed with the dissolution of the League of Nations. The Court advised that South Africa had an international obligation to transmit petitions from the inhabitants of the mandate, and that the U.N. had power to exercise supervisory functions and to receive annual reports and petitions. The degree of supervision, however, should not exceed that applied under the mandate system. It held that South Africa was not obliged to submit the territory to trusteeship—this by a majority of 8 to 6—but that South Africa acting alone lacked competence to alter the international status of the territory. In 1955, the Court advised that the fact the General Assembly reached its conclusions by two-thirds majority, whereas the Council of the League of Nations did so by unanimity, did not alter the extent of supervision over South-West Africa that was permissible. In 1956, the Court advised that the General Assembly's Committee could grant oral hearings to petitioners, even though this had not been done under the League; this was not exercising 'a greater degree of supervision' than under the League, because the League could have thus acted had it so decided.

21. South Africa, for her part, rejected the opinions of 1950 and 1955. Indeed, until the U.N. succeeded in sending the ill-fated Carpio mission to South-West Africa, South Africa refused to heed the International Court in any way over this matter. Then, on 4th November 1960, Liberia and Ethiopia brought the whole case before the International Court of Justice, seeking a ruling upon which the United Nations could act.

22. It must first be noted that the judgment of the Court will be binding on the parties, as it is contentious and not advisory. Ethiopia

and Liberia have asked the Court to adjudicate on three main issues:

(1) To adjudicate that the Union has practised *apartheid* in administering South-West Africa; that this is a violation of Article 2 of the Mandate and Article 22 of the Covenant; and that the Union must cease these practices forthwith.

(2) To declare that the Union has applied in South-West Africa legislation, regulations and administrative decrees which are unjust and unreasonable; that, as such, they are contrary to Article 2 of the Mandate.

(3) To declare that the Union has the duty forthwith to repeal and not to apply legislation coming within the scope of the preceding section.

The application to the Court also takes up certain other points about petitions and the submission of reports to the United Nations on which the Court has already pronounced previous opinions. The purpose of this is to bring them under the umbrella of a binding Court judgment.

23. In December 1962, the Court decided it had jurisdiction to hear the case. It is now hearing the submissions of the parties, and in 1965 will adjudicate on the merits of the case.

24. As the matter is *sub judice*, no presumption should be made as to the Court's findings. But it is wise to consider the hypothesis that the Court will find against South Africa, probably by a wider margin than in the preliminary judgment. Unless it does so, the whole sequence of events at present being prepared for actively by the governments concerned will prove wasted labour. It is prudent, therefore, to examine precisely what may occur in the event of a judgment favourable to Liberia and Ethiopia being handed down next year.

25. It must first be noticed that the Court has not been asked to require specific, positive action by South Africa, but to declare that South Africa has the negative duty of ceasing certain policies and of repealing certain legislation deemed incompatible with her international obligations.

26. South Africa could decide to comply with such a judgment; she could likewise give lip service to the Court, and merely pretend to comply; or she could reject the judgment of the Court.

27. In the last event, Liberia and Ethiopia would have recourse to the Security Council. Article 94 (2) of the Charter provides specifically for such redress.

> If a party to a case fails to perform the obligations incumbent upon it under a judgment rendered by the Court, the other party may have recourse to the Security Council, which may, if it deems necessary, make recommendations or *decide upon measures* to be taken to give effect to the judgment.

28. Under this Article—never before invoked—if the five permanent members of the Security Council were unanimous it could decide upon mandatory measures, including sanctions. The legal basis for such action would be strengthened if the Security Council considered that the very failure to carry out a binding judgment of the Court constituted in this case a threat to peace, thus bringing in Article 39 and Articles 41-42 of the Charter.

29. The unanimity of the permanent members of the Security Council in such a matter would be decisive. This arises from both legal and political reasons:

(*a*) If the veto were used in the Security Council, it is likely the issue would be evoked in the General Assembly. If there were the political will, the Assembly would not be deterred from recommending economic sanctions and the creation of a U.N. force to implement them.[1] But it cannot set up a force, as can the Security Council, to meet a threat to the peace; it has no authority to enforce a decision of the International Court of Justice. The General Assembly can only recommend or express its opinion. Above all, its recommendations are not mandatory. The U.K. would not be bound to participate in any military sanctions recommended by the Assembly. The U.S.S.R. has always denied that any U.N. *force* can be set up under the Uniting for Peace Resolution—even a police force, much less a sanctions force.

(*b*) The essential need for unanimity in the Security Council only illustrates the fact that any enforcement measures must be taken by the major powers. Unless there is Soviet agreement, it cannot be U.N. action, with all the moral and legal authority which the world Organization confers. Unless there is an Anglo-American resolve to implement the Security Council decision, nothing effective could be done anyway. An abstention by France— always possible if that country's policy is to demonstrate the innate superiority of French civilization by seeking every occasion to take an international position different from that of the U.S.A.—would not invalidate a Security Council decision. France, under pressure from her former African colonies, has little incentive to oppose the implementation of any Security Council decision, even though she did not herself participate.

30. Given the hypothesis of a Security Council decision, the position which would then arise has been examined in Section IX of the Report.

---

[1] It is noteworthy that under the Uniting for Peace Resolution, the General Assembly may call for the establishing of a force only if a breach of the peace or act of aggression has actually occurred.

The Odendaal Report

31. In January 1964 a Commission appointed to draw up a five-year development plan for South-West Africa published its 557-page report, in which it recommended the creation of ten separate homelands in South-West Africa, 'which will develop towards self-determination' for the African and Coloured groups in the territory, thus extending to South-West Africa the policy at present being pursued in South Africa.

32. The ten proposed homelands are:

	Population
Ovamboland	239,363
Okavangoland	27,871
Kaokoveld	9,234
East Caprivi	15,840
Damaraland	44,353
Namaland	34,806
Hereroland	35,354
Rehoboth Gebiet	11,257
Bushmanland	11,762
Tswanaland	(not stated)

33. The total area of these territories is to be extended by more than 50 per cent from the present 21,825,997 hectares to 32,629,364 hectares. This total must be compared with the total area of white farms, namely 39,812,000 hectares. In land area, the comparison is 126,000 square miles for the proposed homelands and 192,000 square miles for the white or police area, which includes towns, and game reserves as well as white farms. *The division proposed is thus five-eighths of the land for less than one seventh of the population.* In addition to this inequitable division of land—especially in view of its quality—there is the fact that almost one-third of the non-white population are living in the white area in order to obtain work. In this area, they are subject to the same *apartheid* legislation as in South Africa; thus any African who comes into the white area must carry a work permit or a contract of service or a special permit to be in the area. These must be produced at any time on demand, and failure to produce them is a criminal offence. An African cannot leave his homelands without a pass, nor buy a railway ticket without a special permit. If he has been recruited in one of the homelands for work in the police zone, he is in fact tied to the place of his employment.

34. With regard to the Coloureds (12,708 in number), the Report suggests they be concentrated in Windhoek, Luderitz and Walvis Bay.

35. With these proposals are two five-year development plans, of which the first would cost £78,000,000 and the second £45·5 million, of which £24·5 million will be spent on a hydro-electric scheme on the Kunene river.

36. The basic argument of the Report in favour of the proposals is not the national survival of the white race, as in the Republic, but that 'separate development' is in the best interests of the inhabitants. It is necessary to prove this because the Report proceeds on the assumption that, while the South African Government rejects the view that its administration of South-West Africa is legally governed by the terms of the mandate, nevertheless the administration is conducted in the spirit of the mandate (cp. para. 3). Two reasons are given which conflict. The first is that the most numerous tribe, the Ovambo, which numbers more than 45 per cent of the whole population, would be likely to rule with little consideration for minorities if there were a unitary state with adult suffrage. Such domination would result in 'a lowering of the standard of administration and government, and would also hamper the white, to whom the territory mainly owes its economic progress, to such an extent that the development and progress of the territory would be seriously retarded'. The Report therefore expresses the view that one central authority with all groups represented thereon must be ruled out, and that as far as practicable a homeland must be created for each population group, in which it alone would have residential, political and language rights, to the exclusion of other population groups, so that each group would be 'able to develop towards self-determination without any group dominating or being dominated by another' (paras 189-190.)

37. The second reason given is that for the African population as a whole special measures are needed vis-à-vis the whites, for where population groups are at different stages of socio-cultural advancement, the less advanced will need both protection and special advancement. This is not feasible, it is argued, in an integrated community. 'Where differences are fundamental and so profound that they cannot be wiped out, a policy of integration is unrealistic.' Differentiation, on the other hand, makes possible both advancement and protection (paras 1418-1432). This produces the odd result that, because domination by the Ovambo is eschewed, it is to be preserved for the (much smaller) white group.

38. In political terms, each homeland would have a legislative council, composed of chiefs and headmen, ex officio, but with a limit on the elected members at a maximum of 40 per cent. An executive council would gradually take over the functions of the Department of Bantu Administration and Development, except defence, foreign affairs, internal security and border control, posts, water and power.

39. On the result of these proposals as a whole it has been shrewdly commented:

The argument for giving the whites special treatment in South-West Africa is that they make a special contribution to the economy.

L

As a transitional measure, it is a sound argument, but it can hardly justify giving the whites a privileged position permanently.

True trusteeship would involve training the non-white peoples to make a bigger contribution to the money economy and the removal 'with all deliberate speed' of the racial distinctions in the police or white area. Politically, it would surely mean a steady preparation of the non-white groups for a share, perhaps in a federal system, certainly in one in which all the groups could play a part. It is either disingenuous or naïve to claim that 'one man, one vote' would mean domination of other groups by the Ovambo, and instead to recommend a system whereby domination is, in fact, preserved by the much smaller white group. About three-eighths of the country is to be excised to make homelands for the non-whites, while the rest is left for a white group, not one-seventh of the whole, who in this area have linguistic, political and social rights, just as a Bantu group will have in one of the Bantu homelands, in spite of the fact that even in this area they are outnumbered by more than two to one. To this area, members of other population groups come as contract labourers whose movements are strictly limited, the whole territory, police area and homelands alike, being in fact ruled by the white Government of South Africa—until the day when it is split into eleven self-governing fragments. This is surely white domination, and it is not easy to see how the Ovambo could really improve on the General Laws Amendment Act as an instrument for perpetuating their rule.[1]

40. Certainly the reaction of the Africans has not been left in doubt. Chief Hosea Kutako, the leader of the 35,000 Hereros, and his ten counsellors have condemned the proposals of the Odendaal Commission as an attempt to divide and rule the non-whites, and have stated that they will have nothing to do with the plans and will resist all attempts to resettle their people.

41. Faced with the South African intention of implementing this Report while the South-West Africa case was still *sub judice*, the applicants—Liberia and Ethiopia—considered applying for an interim injunction from the International Court of Justice to prevent this occurring, for fear the feasibility of the due execution of the Court's judgment on merits might be jeopardized (assuming that the judgment would be favourable to the applicants). This would, however, have delayed the final judgment considerably. Nor was the legal position as clear concerning the powers of the Security Council in the event of an interim injunction being granted, as it is in the case of a judgment by the International Court of Justice.

[1] Philip Mason, 'Separate Development and South-West Africa: Some Aspects of the Odendaal Report', *Race*, April 1964.

42. Diplomatic pressure was therefore exerted by the British and American Governments to dissuade the South African Government from implementing the Odendaal Commission's Report pending the judgment of the International Court of Justice.

43. The result of this pressure was a decision by the South African Government announced in a White Paper, published on the 29th April 1964, that it would refrain

> from action which may be regarded—even theoretically—as detrimental or prejudicial to the alleged rights of the applicant states, or which may unnecessarily aggravate or extend the dispute before the Court.

44. In consequence, the South African Government will not implement the recommendation of the Odendaal Commission for the creation of non-white 'homelands' in South-West Africa, pending the Court's judgment, though it will begin to carry out the development schemes proposed in the Report, which envisage total government expenditure of £78,000,000 over a period of five years. The main projects on which immediate action is proposed are water and electricity supplies, road and rail extensions, airfield developments, mining, industrial and agricultural development, education and health services, and the purchase of white-owned land for eventual non-white use if the 'homelands' scheme is implemented. Agricultural development plans include an attempt to introduce groundnut and jute production in Ovamboland. The biggest single project will be the Kunene River development plan, providing both water for the dry months in the northern parts of the territory and electricity for the northern and central parts of the territory at an estimated cost of nearly £25,000,000.

45. The fact that the South African Government responded to this pressure indicates that hopes of pliability with regard to South-West Africa may have some foundation. They are further examined in paragraphs 152-153 of the Report.

XX · THE HIGH COMMISSION TERRITORIES

Area and Location

1. In area, the three Protectorates are over half the size of the Republic (Bechuanaland, 222,000 sq. miles; Basutoland, 11,716 sq. miles; Swaziland, 6,704 sq. miles, i.e. slightly smaller than Wales), though much of Bechuanaland is the Kalahari Desert. A glance at the map shows Basutoland to be entirely surrounded by South African territory, while the other two are bounded by the Republic on three sides.

Population

2. The total population of the huge area of the three Protectorates is only 1,400,000, of which the proportion of Europeans (mostly Afrikaans-speaking) is extremely small. The figures are: Bechuanaland, 350,000; Basutoland, 790,000; Swaziland, 269,000. The proportion of Europeans is respectively 1 per cent, o·3 per cent and 3 per cent. Only Swaziland has a comparatively large and influential minority, numbering some 9,000.

The Economics

3. Agriculture and stock-raising dominate in Bechuanaland and Basutoland, where the farmers have a constant struggle against climate, impoverished soil and a system of land tenure which inhibits the improvement of crop production. In Bechuanaland, 91 per cent of all domestic exports consisted of animal products; in Basutoland, 75 per cent. In Swaziland, there is a substantial sugar industry, which accounts for 30 per cent of export earnings, and an expanding forestry enterprise.

4. Unlike the other two Protectorates, Swaziland has rich mineral deposits, particularly asbestos and iron ore. There are also copper, nickel and cobalt deposits. Asbestos accounts for 62 per cent of export earnings, while the iron ore mine at Bomvu Ridge has now begun operations, and will use the railway which is being built to Goba in Mozambique, to export to Japan.

5. Industry in Basutoland is minimal: one small brickfield and two missionary printing works. In Bechuanaland there is a soap factory, a maize mill and an abattoir at Lobatsi, and a bone-meal factory at Francistown.

British Aid

6. In 1960 an Economic Survey Mission reported:

> Each territory is in the situation of a patient confronted with a choice between having an expensive operation, which would entail a long period of recuperation but offer high chances of full recovery, and the alternative of lapsing into a state of chronic illness.[1]

This comment—coming fifteen years after the war—is a most severe criticism of the amount and effectiveness of British aid, even though this has been more generous than during the inter-war period. Thus under the Colonial Development and Welfare Act of 1955 Bechuanaland and Basutoland received just over £1½ million each, and Swaziland £930,000. The 1959 Act reversed the proportion: Swaziland was to receive £1,750,000; Bechuanaland and Basutoland £750,000 each. In addition, during the ten years 1945-55, loans from the Colonial Development Corporation amounted to £1,350,000.

---

[1] *Basutoland, Bechuanaland Protectorates and Swaziland: Report of an Economic Survey Mission* (H.M.S.O., London, 1960).

7. Nevertheless, today only Swaziland is a potentially viable unit; and this is due in part to the decision taken by business interests, not the Government, to build a railway line. In Basutoland, U.K. aid was needed to the extent of 40 per cent of all government expenditure in 1961-62; in Bechuanaland, nearly £1,000,000 was needed to balance the account. The lack of transport, of power supplies, of water, and the almost nonexistent internal markets, owing to the low level of purchasing power, inhibit progress.

8. This explains why economic aid to the three territories has long been a concern of the British Council of Churches, which addressed its first resolution on this subject to the Government in 1951. In 1963 the Council underlined the link between economic difficulties and political future, calling for

> a policy of vigorous action both to increase the economic viability of the Territories through grants-in-aid and the encouragement of capital investment, to further their self-government and security.

Links with South Africa

9. These can scarcely be exaggerated, and are an important consideration for the British Government in deciding its attitude towards current proposals for economic sanctions being studied by the expert committee set up by the Security Council in June 1964.

10. First, all the Protectorates are in a customs union with the Republic, and by virtue of the 1910 agreement receive a share of its receipts. These amount to half the annual revenue of Basutoland, a quarter of the revenue of Bechuanaland, and 10 per cent of the revenue of Swaziland.

11. Second, the Republic is both the main market and main source of supplies for the three Protectorates. Basutoland's exports are totally directed to the Republic, and more than half of Bechuanaland's. Swaziland has diversified her trading outlets in respect of iron ore and wood pulp. The import situation is that Basutoland and Swaziland are totally dependent on South Africa; in Bechuanaland, 76 per cent of recorded imports came from South Africa in 1960. The essential point among these imports is food. Bechuanaland now imports 125 lb. of maize per head per annum; Basutoland, 67 lb. of maize per head per annum. Without these imports the situation would be difficult indeed.

12. Thirdly, the Republic employs a significant proportion of the Protectorates' labour. The figures are very high: 43 per cent of all Basuto adult males are employed in South Africa; for Bechuanaland and Swaziland the percentages are 20 and 8 respectively. In figures this means 150,000 Basuto, 15,000 Bechuana[1] and 8,500 Swazi are at present work-

[1] A bad crop year in 1963 has increased this number by a further 13-14,000 at the time of writing.

ing in the Republic, mostly in the gold mines of the Transvaal and Orange Free State. The total contribution in terms of remittances, deferred pay, etc., to the revenue of the Territories is of the order of £1,900,000 per annum.

13. It is to be noted that this removal of the bulk of the ablebodied labour force creates a vicious circle, since it leaves agriculture to the children, the women and the aged. This not only prevents agricultural progress and makes them more dependent on migratory labour to pay taxes, but has disastrous effects on family life. But the Morse Report correctly pointed out that unless, or until, the forces responsible for the poor agriculture are reversed, more and more of the Basuto people will be forced to seek work in South Africa in order to escape poverty at home. South Africa has the strongest incentive to import such labour, as it is its cheapness that makes the mines of the Reef so profitable. By allowing and even encouraging the system of migratory labour, the administration of the Protectorates—and therefore the United Kingdom —are assisting the exploitation of African labour, and reducing the incentive to solve the problems of under-employment in Basutoland and Bechuanaland.

14. Fourthly, all three Territories are dependent on the Republic for transport, posts and telegraphs.

15. In summing up: Basutoland cannot live apart from the Republic; Bechuanaland would find it almost impossible; if Swaziland had to do so, it would greatly set back that country's advance to economic viability.

Vulnerability to South African Action

16. In the event of Britain's participating in a naval blockade to enforce sanctions imposed by the United Nations—an act of internationally outlawing South Africa—South Africa could hold she was entitled to occupy the Protectorates as a measure of retortion, while recognizing that this would involve a direct clash with the United Kingdom. Even without such an irrevocable step, the Republic could exercise an economic stranglehold in the following ways:

> (1) Cutting off imports. Bechuanaland could be fed through Northern Rhodesia (provided the Caprivi Strip is not under South African control); Swaziland exports rice; but Basutoland would present a grave problem. In theory, maize could be air-lifted in, but this would mean South African acceptance of the use of her air space,[1] and there is dubiety about the adequacy of landing

---

[1] In international law inland countries have a right of access to the sea, but the analogous right of access by air has been disputed by Chile vis-à-vis Bolivia. In fact, law would have little to do with a blockade situation, which is in itself an appeal to the arbitrament of (indirect) force.

facilities in mountainous Basutoland for such a large-scale operation.

(2) Exports from the Protectorates could be subject to prohibitive duties. Of these exports, migrant labour is the most important. In the event of unemployment arising from sanctions, many might be sent home, or held as hostages.

(3) South Africa could revoke the 1910 customs agreement, thus cutting off an important source of revenue. However, their receipts would in any case be nil for both Republic and High Commission Territories in the event of a trade embargo.

17. These facts must give a pause to those who believe Britain should take part in total sanctions against South Africa. The High Commission Territories are in fact economic hostages, held by the Republic, just as Basutoland and Swaziland are strategic hostages also. If it may be assumed that the ultimate action of a South African invasion of the Protectorates would not take place, because it would involve war with this country, nevertheless H.M. Government would only envisage sanctions if there had been some stockpiling of vital supplies in the Protectorates before the sanctions were imposed.

18. On the other hand, it must be recognized that this problem is not in essence different from the hardship that any sanctions would cause to Africans within the Republic, of whom substantial numbers are migrant Basutos, Bechuanas and Swazis. African opinion is that these hardships would be accepted in order to end *apartheid*; and that, in relation to their present low standard of living in the High Commission Territories, the difference would not be dramatic.

Progress towards Independence

19. This does not alter the moral evaluation of the situation with regard to sanctions, as, in any event, Britain will continue her military and economic ties. It is, however, true that legally the United Kingdom dilemma in respect of Basutoland, if South Africa took the measures of retortion she would be entitled to take in the event of total sanctions, would be mitigated if in the interval Basutoland has become independent; has become a member both of the Commonwealth and United Nations; and the Basuto representative in the General Assembly has voted in favour of U.N. sanctions. Under the recent London agreement, the independence of Basutoland may be established by 1965-66.

20. However, the attitude of the Basuto leaders is not at all favourable to sanctions. In a letter to *The Times*, published on 19th May 1964 following the independence talks in London, the President of the Basuto National Party, Chief Leabua Jonathan, the Member of the Executive Council for Agriculture, D. L. Majara, and the Leader of the Marema Tlou Freedom Party, S. Matiti, wrote:

An attempt to fight *apartheid* by economic sanctions would probably mean the end of the High Commission Territories and especially the end of Basutoland. . . .

The advocates of sanctions seem to us to make two fatal mistakes. They assume that economic sanctions against South Africa could bring South Africa to her knees in a short time, that the effect would be quick and decisive. But such evidence as we have does not confirm this. Sanctions would probably be a long-drawn-out business, inconclusive against strong South Africa, but meanwhile fatal to the small and comparatively weak High Commission Territories.

Secondly, those who call for sanctions assume that the whites who benefit economically from *apartheid* will run away from Dr Verwoerd when they begin to feel the pinch of sanctions. But what right have people to assume this? On the contrary, the whites, and especially those with no strong political convictions, will probably be forced to get together more closely. The South African Government and its real supporters do not believe in *apartheid* because of money and love of ease. *Apartheid* goes very deep; those who believe in it will fight like fanatics, and they will easily hold the weak ones with them.

We repeat that we Africans in Basutoland hate racialism and *apartheid*, but we will not be stampeded into stupid and ineffective ways of fighting it. We have lived with whites and had our differences with them for more than a hundred years. We have survived, and intend to survive. We will not commit suicide.[1]

21. To a limited degree the issue of relations with South Africa has already been posed by the political refugees, which touches directly the British tradition of asylum. White South Africa is becoming increasingly restive at the use of the Territories by their African opponents, many of whom they allege return as trained saboteurs. This issue was considered during the recent negotiations for the independence of Basutoland. However, the real problem here is Bechuanaland, whose

---

[1] It is true that *The Times* published a reply on 22nd May from *outside* Basutoland. The Minister of Justice of Zambia (M. Mainza Chona) wrote bitterly:

If Chief Jonathan thinks it is impossible or suicidal for Basutoland to boycott South African goods, the worst he should do (as one who hates *apartheid*) is to keep silent. To condemn those trying to help him in fighting racialism is inexcusable. In his letter he does not suggest any alternative method of fighting *apartheid*, nor does he believe that anything should be done to put a stop to the sinful ideology.

But to point to the absence of alternative policy except waiting upon the development of the Bantustans does not remove the unpleasant consequences of economic sanctions for Basutoland, as the leaders of that territory accurately perceive. To deny these is not to strengthen the case for sanctions, but to weaken it. Cp. paras 17 and 18 above.

frontier is 1,800 miles long, whereas that of Basutoland is 368 miles, that of Swaziland 200 miles.

22. Bechuanaland is to hold elections in March 1965 and become independent by the end of the year. In August 1964 Seretse Khama, who is expected to become the first Prime Minister after independence, stated to the United Nations expert committee appointed by the Security Council to study sanctions:

Bechuanaland could not implement sanctions against South Africa, because our trade with the Republic is our life-blood.

23. This explains in part Dr Verwoerd's recent statements. Basically, however, the reason is that the policy of 'separate development' does not make sense unless South Africa can incorporate the three High Commission Territories, which would increase the land allocated to African occupation from 13 per cent to 50 per cent. This explains why all three were included in the original Tomlinson Report in 1956, with its proposal to establish seven Bantustans. In 1961, Dr Verwoerd dismissed the possibility of incorporation in the Republic as incompatible with the British policy of granting independence—which illumines the nature of the 'self-government' envisaged for the Bantustans themselves.[1]

24. The general elections in Swaziland on 22nd-28th June indicate developments which may well lead to quite surprising perspectives. It may be that Swaziland will become another Bantustan, and that the Transkei will become another Swaziland. This would be to take the Bantustan concept far beyond it originators' intentions, but it is something that it may prove difficult to stop. The position in Swaziland is that the new Legislative Council is composed as follows;

the Royalist Imbokodvo Party holds 16 of the 24 elected seats;
the United Swaziland Association, 8 seats;
4 nominated government officials.

This means that 24 of the 28 members of Legislative Council are supporters of Paramount Chief Sobhuza II, who is looking with friendly eyes towards Pretoria. The only serious opposition is Dr Ambrose Zwane's Ngwane National Liberty Congress, which was the only party whose candidates did not lose their deposit in the landslide victory of the Royalist and right-wing parties. The Ngwane Congress has strong Pan-African links, socialist economic policies and trade union connections, which could make labour unrest in the asbestos mines a major political weapon. However, the important thing is the majority in Legislative Council and the authority of Chief Sobhuza. On this, Pretoria may hopefully build.

[1] Though it is true that the 'Bantustan' may develop far beyond what Dr Verwoerd originally intended. 'Too much head of steam in the escape valve?' was a recent significant headline in a South African newspaper, referring to the Transkei.

A United Nations 'Presence'?

25. It has been proposed that a team of U.N. observers should be sent to maintain frontier patrols, and teams of technical experts, together with larger grants of economic aid. The attractiveness of this consists in Britain's sharing her responsibilities. Its disadvantage lies precisely in this fact: these are peculiarly British responsibilities. To slide them off on the United Nations would neither remove them nor guarantee that they would be more wisely shouldered. However, if U.K. participation in sanctions were envisaged, Britain would in fact have internationalized her whole South African commitment. At that stage it would be logical to internationalize her commitment also to the High Commission Territories. U.N. economic experts of the Economic Commission for Africa will in any case be in Basutoland next year.

Additional note to page 133.

There is no doubt the Buccaneers are not appropriate aircraft for purposes of internal repression (though they could terrorize by flying low over villages). The serious point is that they are highly effective naval patrol planes. If South Africa is regarded as an ally in a possible conventional war with the Soviet Union, then they would be valuable to protect the Cape sea routes against Russian submarines or cruisers. If South Africa is regarded as a possible object of United Nations police action, then the selfsame 'planes supplied by Britain could be used against any U.N. force, in which British ships and men would have to take part, if it were ever to be mounted. It is significant for instance that the Simonstown Agreement includes the patrol of the Southern Atlantic ocean off South West Africa. Such perspectives, however, are a long way off, and it is to be hoped will never materialize, because South African racial policies will change. For this change to take place, however, a policy of explicit British dissociation from *apartheid* is essential. The Buccaneer decision cuts right across this, for it means that Britain will be involved militarily with South Africa into the 1970's, because of the undertaking to supply spare parts. It is a decision of deep significance, which may be deeply regretted.

XXI · SELECT BIBLIOGRAPHY

CARTER, GWENDOLEN M.	*The Politics of Inequality: South Africa since 1948* Thames & Hudson, 1961
COWEN, D. V.	*The Foundations of Freedom: with special Reference to Southern Africa* Oxford University Press, 1961
DVORIN, E. P.	*Racial Separation in South Africa: an Analysis of Apartheid Theory* Chicago University Press, 1952
HELIMANN, ELLEN	*Handbook on Race Relations in South Africa* Oxford University Press for the South African Institute of Race Relations, 1949. Brought up to date by the *Annual Survey of Race Relations in South Africa*

DE KIEWIET, C. W. — *The Anatomy of South African Misery*
Oxford University Press, 1956

KRUGER, D. W. — *South African Parties and Policies 1910-1960: a select source book*
Bowes & Bowes, 1960

LEGUM, C. AND M. — *South Africa—Crisis for the West*
Pall Mall, 1964

LUTHULI, ALBERT — *Let my People go*
Collins, 1962

MACCRONE, I. D. — *Race Attitudes in South Africa: Historical, experimental and psychological studies*
Witwatersrand University Press, 1957

MANSERGH, N. — *South Africa 1906-1961: the Price of Magnanimity*
Allen & Unwin, 1962

MARAIS, B. — *The Two Faces of Africa*
Pietermaritzburg, Shuter & Shooter 1964

MARQUARD, LEO — *The Peoples and Policies of South Africa*
Oxford University Press, 3rd edition, 1962

NEAME, L. E. — *The History of Apartheid: the Story of the Colour War in South Africa*
Pall Mall and Barrie & Rockliff, 1962

NGUBANE, JORDAN K. — *An African Explains Apartheid*
Pall Mall Press

PIENAAR, S., and SAMPSON, A. — *South Africa: Two Views of Separate Development*
Oxford University Press for Institute of Race Relations, 1960

RHOODIE, N. J., AND VENTER, H. J. — *Apartheid*
Cape Town, Haum, 1960

ROSKAM, K. L. — *Apartheid and Discrimination*
Leyden, A. W. Sythoff, 1960

SEGAL, R. (Editor) — *Sanctions against South Africa*
Penguin Books, 1964

UNITED NATIONS — *Report of the United Nations Commission on the Racial Situation in the Union of South Africa*
New York, 1953

UNITED NATIONS—*cont.*   *2nd Report of the United Nations Commission on the Racial Situation in the Union of South Africa*
New York, 1954
Report by the Secretary General of 20th April 1964, in pursuance of the Resolution adopted by the Security Council on 4th December 1963

WORLD COUNCIL OF CHURCHES   *Report of Mindolo Consultation on Race Relations in Southern Africa, May 1964*
Selected Addresses given at the above Consultation